DOUBLE HEADER

My Life with Two Penises

DIPHALLIC DUDE

DOUBLE HEADER
My Life With Two Penises
1st Electronic Edition December 2014
COPYRIGHT © 2014 DDD Publishing

DOUBLE HEADER
My Life With Two Penises
1st Paperback Edition December 2016.
COPYRIGHT © 2016 DDD Publishing
ISBN: 978152020

Cover art/photography by DDD.
COPYRIGHT © 2014 DDD Publishing

ALL RIGHTS RESERVED

This book, and/or parts thereof, may not be reproduced in any form without permission. Names, places, people and events have been modified for privacy reasons. The sexuality of individuals in this book are portrayed as the authors opinion and are not to be understood as an assertion of fact. Some details and facts have been removed or altered during editing to protect the author and his identity. Some portions of this book feature quotes, questions or other written public elements originating from individuals on the Internet and are considered fair use; crediting is given when possible.

For author information including photography of DDD's anatomy visit:

www.twitter.com/DiphallicDude
www.diphallicdude.tumblr.com

DEDICATION

To all the fantastic, funny and weird people I've encountered on the internet. Never did I think during that wild Ask Me Anything on Reddit would I end up having impacted so many people. To those who consider themselves misfits, weirdos, awkward or otherwise "different" people; this print edition is for you. You're not alone.

CONTENTS

1	Diphallia	Pg 1
2	Growing Up	Pg 3
3	Exposed	Pg 6
4	Too Much of a Good Thing?	Pg 11
5	Bad-Ass	Pg 13
6	Owning the D's	Pg 16
7	A Brand New World	Pg 19
8	Clearing Up Confusion	Pg 21
9	All About the D's	Pg 25
10	Everything You Wanted to Know	Pg 48
11	Funny Moments	Pg 55
12	Ye' Ole' Prostate	Pg 62
13	The Orgy	Pg 66
14	10 Favorites From My Reddit AMA	Pg 70
15	What Started It All	Pg 73
16	Tumblr Fun	Pg 84
17	Notes From DDD	Pg 95
18	In Closing…	Pg 97

A NOTE FROM DDD:
(Updated from electronic version)

When I 'came out' to the world on Reddit, I had no idea anyone would really care that much about me. When you've had two dicks your whole life, it's not a big shock. Fascination about my double dicks is one thing. However it's the wave of acceptance for being myself that inspired me to write this book. I'll try to cover all the bases. When I first wrote the electronic version of this book I found it difficult writing about myself. Especially in such a revealing way. Special thanks to the editor/publisher who stuck by me during the original editing process. They gave me this chance to get my story out. In my own words, on my own terms, with no risk of losing my anonymity. They agreed to let me control what was edited and how things were formatted. They waived all credits for publishing and signed all sorts of legal agreements that protect me. This is something almost no one else has offered. In exchange, I've relinquished all proceeds and profit from the sales of this book to them. Money was never the motivating factor for writing this book. In reality my privacy was the one thing holding me back. My privacy is extremely important. Imagine if Superman went public as Clark Kent. His life would never have been the same. The same applies to me. I like walking amongst everyone else knowing they have no idea who I am. This book will give you a chance to walk in my shoes and maybe when you've finished reading it, you'll understand why being the man with two penises isn't exactly what you thought it would be.

Then again, maybe you will.

Love, DDD

DIPHALLIA

Guess what? A condition that has been linked to legends, myths, humorous stories, movies and now crummy television shows actually exists! The reality is that most cases of diphallia (pronounced: die-fal-ee-ah) are pretty damn brutal (I'm talking life threatening okay?). A lot of boys don't live long after birth.

Without getting technical diphallia really jacks up the body. Spina bifida and a handful of other nasty conditions usually accompany diphallia. The most minor cases give the baby boy a duplicate penis that may or may *not* work. It may not be fully functional and it might just look like a growth. However some have two working, but not very 'attractive' penises. So when my parents discovered that their third child appeared to be suffering from something potentially life threatening, they were terrified. To put it simply, two dicks were the *least* of their concerns.

You see, my mother had two previous miscarriages. I have two siblings, in the ground. So when they discovered she was pregnant again they were worried. The cause of my diphallia isn't one they can pinpoint. Medically the explanation is that she suffered some sort of trauma or stress during my initial development. Exactly what it was is not certain since the first signs of my diphallia were there in the ultrasound when she first went in to be examined. There wasn't a point when my second penis appeared, so linking it to a specific incident is impossible. All they could do was hope and pray that I wouldn't end up showing more complications as the pregnancy continued. Leading up to my birth my mother had regular check-ups and besides having two dicks, they saw no other problems in the ultrasounds. Even still, they were all concerned.

I was born in the summer of 1989. My father explained that when I came out the doctor heaved a sigh of relief and announced:

"It's a boy!"
To which one of the midwives exclaimed: "Boy oh BOY is it a boy!"
There was a sigh of relief and then the doctor announced:
"Ten fingers, ten toes and well, hot damn, two penises, just like we expected!"

Since my penises were both fully formed and functional my parents decided to 'leave things be.' I remember at some point in my youth my mother explained that I had two for a reason so she and my father saw no need to remove one. Looking back over the documents that I've seen, it might have also been because both penises were almost equal in size and pretty difficult to determine which was the duplicate and which was the original.

To this day I still don't know if the right one or left one was the original. The right one is still the strongest and most durable but that could be simply due to blood flow. The world may never know! It's my bet they grew simultaneously.

GROWING UP

Still one of the biggest, if not the most frequent question I've been asked is when did I realize I was "different" from other boys. The answer unfortunately isn't very interesting; I don't know really. Ever since I can remember I knew I was special. My mother made sure at some point (before I could remember), to drill it into my brain that I was special and different from other boys. Both my parents made it very clear to me that I was not to tell other people I had two penises. I can't really put into words my mind-set then.

As I got older my mother made it clear to me that I shouldn't tell anyone because it might make other boys feel bad that they only had one penis. I do remember my mother telling me once never to play "doctor" with my friends. Which by the way I did have to avoid. Boys and girls are really curious about that stuff. The bottom line was, however they explained it then, it stuck with me. I was never, ever made to feel 'different' or 'abnormal.' I always felt like I was special. Also, not special in the way teenagers identify as only something a parent would say. I really *did* feel special. Almost like a super hero as goofy as it might sound.

Puberty came and I noticed that my right dick was

growing a bit bigger than my left one. Up to that point they had been relatively equal in size. I also was having wet dreams very early. My mother took me in to the doctor for my annual check-up. I remember the scene vividly. It was the first time I really got a grasp on how unique I really am. For some reason my personal doctor was not there that day and another doctor came in to see me. One look and he said he'd be back in a moment. The next thing I knew the door was wide open and a handful of other people were with him coming into the room.

A few things happened all at once. A few gasps came out of the group, my mother threw a sheet over my lap and proceeded to shove the group out of the room. I didn't really hear what the man was saying as he stuttered at my mom. All I really remember is her slapping him in the face while telling him "My son is not a freak show!"

GO MOM!

Up to that point it never really seemed like having two dicks was that big of a deal. Sure I felt special, and unique as I grew older. But in the early years it was all I knew. I guess my advice is to try imagine it like having a belly button that pokes out instead of in, or the other way around. It's just how things are.

I handled them the way any other guy handles one dick (no pun intended). I didn't talk about them or bring attention to them. They are just part of me. Elementary life was fine. I was never really bullied or made fun of. I did well in school and progressed into high school. Where we lived it went from elementary directly into high school with five grades all in the same school. I avoided most sports, not because I didn't like sports, or because I wasn't capable of participating. I just had no desire to play anything. I enjoyed music and art more than anything else.

DOUBLE HEADER: MY LIFE WITH TWO PENISES

Locker room situations didn't exist for me because I wore briefs under my boxers for the days when we were to change into gym clothes. Up until nearly the end of my 10th grade year I had successfully managed to keep my double dicks hidden from sight. No one knew... Yet.

EXPOSED

She was nice and I thought she was pretty. It wasn't until after the fact that I realized, she talked, a lot. We had 'dated' a few times. Kissed once or twice and held hands. I was awkward for sure. She had been very interested in having sex. I got excited about the idea but it wasn't until I really thought about it that it became clear that it might not go well. Or at least it wouldn't be like anyone else's first time. I was so accustomed to my life that I didn't factor in what would happen when she saw both my dicks.

I kept avoiding the entire ordeal. I was 16, I had my driver's license and was able to use our spare truck to go to school. She had been on me about going camping before it got cold. I did a pretty good job of putting it off until late spring of the following year. Tenth grade was wrapping up in a few weeks and I kept feeling like it was a bad idea. What most guys would have been going crazy for, had me nervous and paranoid. Spring break of that year is when it happened. Going into a lot of detail is still difficult for me.

We had been drinking (yes I was under age, when did that stop anyone?) and I was really relaxed about everything. After half a bottle of butterscotch schnapps everything seemed great. We were parked not too far from her house and had thrown an air mattress and sleeping bags in the back. She had long since stopped pushing me for sex. So I literally had no idea she had other plans. I laid there staring up at the almost night sky when suddenly I felt her hands trailing down below my waist. Before I could say anything she noticed. I froze up and held my breath. She would be the first person to ever see them that wasn't a doctor or my parents. She didn't react really. She smiled and seemed amused.

I lost my virginity. It didn't bother me really. I had never thought I'd save myself for marriage. I just had never thought I'd have sex any time "soon." So when it happened I shrugged it off. Things seemed to stay normal for the first few days back at school. It was probably the second week after Spring Break that I noticed girls were looking at me a little more frequently than usual. They also stared at my crotch a lot more than I was used to. To give you an idea of how oblivious I was, it hadn't crossed my mind that she told anyone. Boy was I wrong.

I usually gave my buddy a ride home after school. He hated riding the school bus and lived only a street passed mine. It was on the ride home when it all came full circle. I still remember it like it was yesterday. Another defining moment in my youth.

"So is it true?"

I looked over at him while sitting at the stoplight.

"Is what true?"
"There's a rumor going around right now that you've got two dicks."

It felt like my stomach went straight through the floor.

"Who the heck is saying that?"

He got quiet, then asked me.

"No one has two dicks." I tried dodging the question.
"Show me."

That really caught me off guard.

"You want me to show you my dick?" I tried to deflect again.
"If you have only one, then prove it."

I really couldn't figure out what to do so I just laughed at him and told him he was nuts. The rest of the ride to his house was in silence. If he kept insisting, I had no idea what I was going to say or do. I tried figuring out how I could pull one out through the fly of my pants without showing the other one. By the time we were pulling into his driveway I had figured if I was really careful about it I could probably pull the right one out and he'd be satisfied enough.

"Keeping secrets and stuff like that isn't cool. I've told you practically everything I've ever even *thought* about."

He was right. We'd been friends for years. He was mad and I felt really bad. Not bad enough though.

"Here," I sighed as I managed to get my fly open and pull out only my right dick.

He glanced over and looked at it and then back up at my face.

"Unzip your pants and show me the whole package."

My stomach fell again. He was a lot smarter than I had

expected.

I started to tuck it away when he practically demanded it.

I'm not sure if it was the tone of his voice, or the hurt and betrayed look on his face that made me feel bad. Before I even realized what my hands were doing, both of my dicks were out, right there in the truck.

"Daaaaamn," he sort of whispered as he leaned over and stared down at them.

"So she told *everyone*?"

Without looking away from them he replied.

"A few of her friends, but it's getting around. I don't think anyone believes her though."

I felt myself getting hard and immediately put them away and zipped up my pants.

"You can't tell anyone."

He looked at me and it was pure confusion.

"Why not? Are you kidding you'll rule over all the jocks!"

I felt like smiling. The warning my parents gave me had lasted that long and I found myself shocked that he wasn't upset or angry that he had only one! That warning I grew up with seemed to be in error. At least with him.

"No, you've got to promise you won't tell anyone."
After arguing with him about my reasons for keeping it secret I left and went home hoping that he wouldn't tell anyone. Little did I know he ended up wrecking his own

identity to protect mine.

Half way through the next day I started hearing guys talking about my buddy. The gossip was he was a queer. Not only that but somehow I was too. I caught up with him after lunch and asked him what the hell he said. Believe it or not, he was mad, at me.

"I defended you, I told the guys who were talking about you that you didn't have two dicks."

Before I could smile he kept talking.

"They wanted to know how I knew and I said that you showed it to me and now suddenly I'm a faggot."

I felt my fists clenching up. Not only had he kept my secret, he lied for me too. In return he was being treated like shit by the other guys.

"You can't say or do anything, they'll just demand you prove it and you can't."

That's when it all started going downhill.

I glossed over this part in my Reddit AMA. It's not really easy to explain all this when you're getting thousands of questions shot at you all at one time. The fact is I have two dicks, the word got out and my friend tried to protect me. Before we were prepared for it, we were both labeled 'gay.' I also have to admit I wasn't really forthright with some of my replies in the AMA. I never showed my cocks in school, even when people started talking about them. I had a long discussion with my family about them. The fact was, I wanted one of them removed. I wanted to only have one dick, like everyone else. I did not want the attention, especially because it was very confusing how each person was acting differently.

TOO MUCH OF A GOOD THING?

Somehow I convinced myself that having one cut off would make everything better. What had made me special, made me miserable. I couldn't prove the bullies wrong. I went from being "cool" during the first week. When my buddy tried to save me from persecution we were labeled "faggots." I went from being the cool taboo dude who supposedly had two dicks, to the queer who probably didn't have two dicks. In one fail swoop he gave them another, more accepted target. Sexuality. It was more fun to call us homo's than it was to focus on something that made me (in the high school mentality) superior to them.

One day near the end of the year I came home with a bruised up hand. My parents had received a call from the school that I had gotten into another fight. What seems to be another difference about myself from what I've seen a lot is that I didn't back down from bullies. I stood up and fought back. Some people are just more meek than others. I definitely wasn't meek about being pushed around. Honestly I was just sick of people being rude for no reason. I was sick of being treated badly after so many years of just fading into the scenery. I was convinced I'd figured out how to handle it. I was sitting in the car with my dad when I told him I wanted one of my dicks cut off. It was going to be the left one, I was ready for it to go. (Sorry Lefty!)

"I know *why* you want this. I really do. But even if you do, you'll still be the guy they make fun of. You'll still be the gay guy who might or might not have had two dicks," my dad replied calmly.

Since I hadn't shown anyone except my buddy and the girl I lost my virginity to, it was her word against his. My buddy was labeled gay and she ended up getting labeled a slut. Somehow I fucked up two people's lives just because I had two dicks. After talking with my dad about it more, it became obvious that cutting one off wasn't going to do any good. It all clicked when he said something that I'll never forget.

"Don't let the bastards get you down. You've got one up on all of them. To hell with the jealous fucks."

When I told him that they said I was gay he laughed and said something else amazing.

"What does that matter? If you are, you are, if you aren't you aren't. You're still my boy and whatever or whoever you like doesn't matter. I don't think you even know what you like yet. So don't let that bother you either. Your mother and I love you no matter what. Ignore those bastards."

As you read this now it's worth mentioning that my father has passed away. He died not too long after I went 'public' and after I initially had written this portion. Having to go back to this spot and edit it only shows me how much he meant to me. His memory lives on with me. I hope this reaches those of you who don't think a father like that exists. They do. Mine did and I'm a better person for it.

BAD-ASS

From that point on I continually got into trouble. I never really went out of my way to cause it. Seriously, I wasn't looking for trouble. But at the same time I never backed down from it. My buddy and I got closer as friends. He nicknamed me "Double D." To say that the school got really tired of my shenanigans was putting it mildly. By the beginning of my senior year I had all but been expelled. Something that really frustrates me, even to this day is the mentality the school had. I was the one being bullied, yet I got punished just as much as the bullies because I stood up for myself.

How can any mature human being fault someone for defending themselves? I get punched, I'll punch back. The idea of rolling over and taking it never existed for me. Well, not until later on, in the bedroom anyway. But that's for later in the book.

My parents and I were called into the principal's office to have a meeting. I was on the edge of expulsion and I really wanted to graduate. The compromise was half days. I'd avoid confrontation as much as possible and I could leave at lunch and go home. This bummed out my buddy since he had to stay on for the full day schedule. I found out after school that a lot of the guys really did think I was gay because I would come pick my buddy up after school to prevent him from being bullied on the bus. He never stood up for himself and was always persecuted. I felt I had to do whatever I could to help him avoid that. After all, it was my fault he was being treated like shit.

So the senior prom was out. I had absolutely no desire to be around any of those people by that point. It wasn't until the following Monday that I heard the news. The girl I lost my virginity to had been killed in a car wreck on the night of senior prom. I am leaving out the details purposefully. All I can say is, I felt a twinge in my stomach when I heard the news. I didn't show up to her funeral as I avoided just about everyone I knew from school. All I know is that I wish I could have said something to her to tell her I didn't think she was a slut, or weird for having sex with me. I just wished she hadn't told anyone, somehow I think she probably wished the same thing.

Graduation came and went. I didn't go, I received my diploma in the mail and it was all over and done with. No walk down the aisle, no tossing the hat in the air. My parents took me and my buddy out to dinner and then it was all over. Suddenly school was in my past. It was weird not having to deal with school anymore. No more early mornings. No more trying not to fall asleep during first period. Suddenly all the faces that either taunted me, or looked at me warily were no longer a part of my life. People I saw every day, people I avoided or were tormented by literally vanished from my 'reality.' An entirely new world was opening up.

That's something important that everyone should know, who hasn't experienced it yet. Especially teens. Considering the content of this book I don't know how many teenagers will read this but it's important that they know. All that shit doesn't matter in the real world. The grief other kids give you, the needless insanity, all that will go away. You just have to hold out long enough. Those jerks worth screwing yourself up over, or even worse, ending your own life. I had some seriously dark moments in my final months of high school. As you already know I had wanted to have one of my dicks cut off. I can see why other guys and girls at that age would think about suicide.

Don't do it!

The people causing you that pain aren't worth your life, your soul and immortality. Yeah, I'm Christian and I believe there's more beyond death. You don't have to believe that, that's your choice. But what if there is? Suicide is just going to close that door forever. Anyway, I'll move on from religion. It's not popular and it's entirely because of the people who follow it, not the message under it all; which is love.

Just remember, treat everyone the way you want to be treated. Don't bully someone, or give someone grief just because you feel like shit. What hurts you, hurts me, what scars your heart, scars others. Why leave a negative mark on another person? Especially when you can do so much more for them by being kind. It's worth thinking about. Just remember, good comes back to you whenever you put it out there. No matter where you send goodness and love, it will find its way back to you. It may not happen tomorrow and it may not come back from the person or place you sent it. But trust me when I tell you, it always will come back to you.

OWNING THE D'S

Okay so this is probably where a lot of you will really start enjoying my story. After my AMA on Reddit it became really obvious to me that something I live with is something very "wow." I have to admit, having two dicks *is great*. I'm so glad I have them. If I looked down tomorrow and saw only one, it would freak me out.

So here we come to sexuality. It's been asked if having two dicks made me bisexual. Or if I'd be straight if I only had one dick. I can't answer either of those really because I've always had two dicks. Since one didn't just appear one day, I have no context of life without two. Now, being bisexual was something I didn't choose. It was something I just happened to notice. As far back as my single-digit years I remember getting boners looking at both guys and girls. It was never predictable. Sometimes there are periods of time where I find myself only attracted to girls, and other times I find myself only attracted to guys. The point is I like both but didn't realize just how much I liked both until I'd had sex with both.

As I mentioned I lost my virginity in high school to a girl. This leads into the question: With which dick? My right one. Up until the summer of 2014 it was always the one I favored the most. I'm right handed so that may be why. However it wasn't until I had sex with my buddy (yeah it happened) that I realized I really do like both guys *and* girls.

I was 18 and with the hell of high school behind me, to be blunt, I wanted to fuck. I'd now had sex with a girl and a guy and really enjoyed how it felt. Now as reckless as I ended up getting, I had seen how people were posting photos on websites and text messages on cell phones. I knew the second I did that, I'd have to deal with being known everywhere I went. So I decided that I'd keep them a secret until I was ready to reveal them. My buddy thought it was probably mean to "unleash" them on those random unsuspecting people. But we agreed that the reactions would be priceless. Also, who would ever believe anyone?

"I sucked off a guy with two dicks last night!"
"Sure you did..."
"No really he had two big uncut dicks!"
"Pics or it didn't happen."

BOOM. Problem solved.

So somewhere there are a lot of people going, "I TOLD YOU! I FUCKING TOLD YOU!"

The question you're probably wondering is just how much I 'owned' them. Honestly, more than I should have. Since I had gotten so much grief from people who never saw them I felt justified in my desires to have people want them. The biggest difference though was between men and women. In retrospect I realized I really enjoyed showing them to guys more than girls. I guess it always felt a little mean to be rude about them when a girl was involved. When it was a guy, I liked seeing them stare and gawk and get that uncomfortable look that almost always lead to them actually doing something with them. The best way to put it, is as follows:

With girls:

"You don't have to touch them, it's cool."

With guys:

"TOUCH THEM! SUCK THEM! You KNOW you want to!"

So I guess the treatment in high school sort of caused that kind of mind-set. Since guys had been more verbally abusive, subconsciously I wanted to see a guy go against his "better judgement" and do what I told him. Or even better, do what he secretly wanted to do.

For clarification, I have never once forced them on anyone. That's not saying I didn't command a number of guys to do what I wanted. The truth is, it's much more fun when the person actually wants to partake in something, even if they're not sure they should. Forcing someone is not only wrong, it's totally disgusting and anyone who does that should be locked up for a long, long time without a key.

A BRAND NEW WORLD

So with high school over, everything was different. I had a few different jobs for a few months. Nothing interesting, at least interesting enough to write about. From a grocery store bag boy, to working at a drive-in movie theater to a car wash. The real interesting stuff started when I met a woman in her 40's who became my sugar momma. Yes, they do exist.

It was the end of the summer, I'd just turned 19 and was ready to get out of the house. She was too classy to ask for sex. But I gave her a lot of eye-candy. She told me how her grandmother remembered a man with two dicks many, many years ago. She had thought there was no such thing until she saw my bulges the day she brought her car in to be washed. My shorts had gotten wet and she noticed the outlines. From that day on I earned a steady income as her house boy. I worked for her almost full time for six full months. She lived about an hour away from my home in the city and allowed me to stay in her guest house as part of payment for taking care of odds and ends at her home.

Somewhere in the sixth month her mother suffered a stroke and died. She had to leave for Florida to help with arranging her estate and left me to watch over her house.

Looking back, she should have known better. She was gone for almost two months and during that two months I probably had a party every week. Nothing ever got broken, but that place saw more sex than I think it had ever seen before. It all ended when she returned during one of the parties. I was on my back with a girl riding my face while a guy had his arm up my ass when suddenly the girl got off my face and I looked over.

"It's time for you to find a new place to live."

She didn't say anything other than that. The party ended, everyone left. I cleaned up the place by the next morning. She returned and handed me an envelope and I got in a cab and left. There was a small note that said something to the effect of "I wish you well, stay safe and call you mother more often," along with a check to me for fifty thousand dollars. Needless to say, I didn't have to move home. I found out not too long ago that she has since passed away as well. A lot of chapters are closed from those years of my life. I'll try to do them justice in the coming 'pages.' Seeing it in print feels weird and I guess, unrealistic to some. But it was my life.

CLEARING UP CONFUSION

I could spend chapters and chapters writing about every nuance of my daily life. Where I moved to, how I lived and what I did to fill spare time. If I did that I'd risk having this book being critiqued as 'boring.' I lived just about the same as any guy my age did. The only difference is the obvious one. So I'll stick to the 'interesting' parts of it all. As I've mentioned in various places on the Internet, in my AMA etc, I got a little carried away with having two dicks at one point.

I thought about becoming an adult entertainment performer. I don't call them actors, because they're not acting, they're fucking. I'm sure some will take offense to my saying so. The fact remains, really no talent is involved in being a 'porn' star. You either have a great face and body and good equipment, or you don't. It's glorified prostitution, only the people paying you aren't the ones you're having sex with (most of the time). I got offers here and there from people claiming to have connections. I refused to allow anyone to take a photo and I turned down a lot of interview requests.

Looking back now, I'm really glad I did. The exposure from my Reddit AMA was overwhelming. I told my boyfriend and girlfriend during the final hours that I felt like I needed to hide under the bed. I was on the front page of so many websites and news sites. It freaked me out. So you can only imagine what going into porn a few years back might have caused.

The truth of the matter is, I love sex. I guess it makes sense when you've got twice as much 'tackle' to work with. In the beginning I generally only used the right one for penetration. Lefty took some serious attention to get hard enough to penetrate someone who wasn't very loose. Thankfully since the corrective surgery and re-alignment I went through back in February of 2014, both right and left now get almost equally hard in almost the same time. So they are equal opportunists!

Back to the point of this section. I love sex, I love sex with women, with men, with men and women at the same time. The prudes might have a tough time in the coming chapters/sections because I'm not a 'polite' descriptor when it comes to things that turn me on. Example? Sure! I love sucking a dick while mine are plowing away inside someone. It doesn't matter if they're inside a woman, or a man, just pounding them in while a cock fills my mouth really does it for me. See what I mean? Nothing delicate about that description! So if that's too much for you, you might want to rethink continuing this book. If you made it through that without feeling disgusted, awesome!

The fact is from the first time I had sex with a guy I knew I liked it. The smell and touch of another guy triggers something in me that doesn't happen with women. Still, the same thing can be said about women, there's just something so different about both that I crave and desire, beyond the physical. I'll try to explain it and hopefully maybe put some real words behind what I think most bisexual people feel. Since we 'bi' people have been called confused, cowards, greedy and slutty, I feel someone should stand up for us.

DOUBLE HEADER: MY LIFE WITH TWO PENISES

First of all, I am not confused. I can't speak for all people who consider themselves bisexual. However, I can speak for myself and if it rings true for others, fantastic. Again, I am not confused, I know exactly what turns me on and what I am attracted to.

I am not a coward, I'm not too afraid to come out as gay, living as bisexual. I don't know many gay men who'd do what I've done with women. That's putting it as politely as I can.

I am not greedy. That implies that I just want it all. I only want specific things.

I am not slutty. That implies I have no standards. If there's no attraction, there's no action.

I can't tell you how many gay men and women have told me I was a confused, greedy little slut, too cowardly to just come out as gay. I've also had a few straight friends accuse me of being greedy or slutty. What may come as a surprise is that I have more straight friends than gay friends, which stems from poor treatment from the gay community. Without taking up an entire feature length portion of this book, I'll simply state that the gay community needs to get it's shit together before it starts demanding anything from the straights. Get your house in order before you start demanding equal treatment. If you want it, you better show it to those of us you've condemned as confused cowards.

Women, I love them. The way they smell, the feel of their body the smoothness of their skin. Cupping a pair of breasts while kissing my way across her collar bone to her ear is heaven. The curve of a woman's hips and the way they feel in my hands when I'm doing the business is intoxicating. The femininity, vulnerability, delicate features, tenderness and sweetness of a woman makes me go wild inside. Not to mention I really love a sexy pussy. Sorry, but it's true. A sexy pussy isn't just a standard 'type' of pussy. I've seen them all. Big and tan, worn out and gaping, to tiny and tight, pink and virginal. Smooth, hairy, landing strip, triangle... Big labia, small labia, non-existent labia, monstrously huge and hanging labia, I love them. Giant clits, to tiny clits, huge pee-holes to tiny pee-holes, I've licked them. To any girls/ladies/women reading this, please stop worrying about what your pussy looks like. It's your pussy, don't let anyone tell you it's not perfect.

Men? Yeah, I love them. The scent of their body, the strength in their muscles curls my toes. I love brushing my lips along a strong jaw-line. It might have a dusting of hair, rough and prickly. It might be smooth like velvet, following it back behind his ear... RAWR! The masculinity of a sexy man turns on a switch inside me that makes me want to wrestle him down and dominate him. It could be from being treated like crap by the jerks in my last years of high school. Not sure, but I love being dominant over a guy. However there are times where I like goofing around the way gay porn has depicted frat jocks. I love ass as well. From the slender twink butt to the beefy jock butt. Giving it a smack before stuffing it full of my cocks... love it. As for cocks, size, shape, etc. don't mean much to me. From big throbbing uncut cocks covered in a thick foreskin with huge rippling veins, to slender circumcised cocks, pale with a pink head, they are fun. Size doesn't matter, the right person won't care, if they care, they're not the right person.

So now that we've gotten that established, if you're still with me I think you're ready for some of my adventures. Afterward I'll review a few things I learned, answer the top 20 most asked questions. For those who missed it I'll include the top questions I answered in my Reddit AMA. Hopefully you will feel this was worth your time. If not, I can't apologize, all I can be is me. Take it or leave it.

ALL ABOUT THE D'S

So what's it like having two dicks? It's great, especially if you're bisexual. Why is that? Well sure, a straight guy would love to have them too. Come on, the women, let me tell you about the women! Right? Yeah not so much. You see, it's been my experience that when it comes to having two working dicks, most women think you're joking, or they flat out refuse. I'd say on average, 6 out of 10 women wouldn't go all the way. The funny thing is, when it comes to having two dicks, the men are where most of the surprising and unexpected action happens. In most cases, all 10 out of 10 men go farther than those 6 women who wouldn't. I saw some guys disagreeing with this when I stated it in various places during and after my AMA. So I'll clarify, 10 out of the 10 men I've been in a potentially sexual situation with, went from potentially sexual, to a completely sexual situation. That's not saying that every man wants to have sex with me, it means the ones who've seen my dicks, did something with them. Maybe that just means I'm good at 'reading' guys and I only get into those situations with men that I know will give them a try. Either way, I stand by my statement. Which brings us to the jock in the gym that I mentioned in my AMA. During the AMA there was no time to give much detail to anything briefly summarizing the Gym Dude.

GYM DUDE
(A highly explicit gay encounter, not for the faint of heart.)

I had a membership to one of those 24 hour, 7 days a week gyms. Most times I'd come in and work-out in the evenings, for a few reasons. At night, there's less traffic and more machines and equipment are available. Also there's less risk of an awkward moment in the locker room. Most nights I'd get in around 3AM and would have the run of the mill. However from time to time there would be at least one other person pumping iron. Since I didn't go to the gym to pick up men or women I never went in anything remotely flattering. I've got a few pairs of mesh shorts with a liner, some standard white jockstraps and a variety of logo t-shirts. I'd throw in a change of clothes in the chance I'd have an empty locker room to change in. On the evening in question I had gotten in a little before 2AM and the gym was dead empty. During my cardio warm up on the treadmill I noticed an unfamiliar face come in, an attractive one at that.

He was roughly 5 foot 10, stacked with muscles and nicely tan. His dirty blond hair was shaggy enough to cover his ears and fall in his green eyes. Tan with just the right amount of vascular definition to catch my attention. I love a nice vein on a bicep, what can I say? I noticed him in the mirrors as he walked by and nodded at him. He smiled briefly and went into the locker room. I came off the treadmill and headed for the free weights to start my standard routine. I tend to lose track of time when I'm working out. I get lost in the music on my MP3 player and before I know it a solid two hours is up and I'm ready to leave. Halfway through my pec-fly's I noticed him looking at me again. The entire wall to my left was completely mirrored and I happened to glance that way to see him staring down in my lower crotch area. I tend to sit spread eagle from time to time so I figured he'd noticed a bulge. I also realized that I had managed to pop out of both sides of my jockstrap. Yeah, I was aware that it was happening while I was going through my routine. But you have to remember, normally I'm alone when I'm working out so I didn't stop to reach in and stuff my dicks back in place.

As usual, in certain situations when the risk of drawing too much attention isn't a threat I decided to be a tease. I got up and strolled over to the leg press. Since my dicks had only just worked their way out of either side, standing and walking caused them to fall completely out of my jock strap. I threw on a few plates, squatted down to tie my shoe, knowing he was watching my every move. After getting into position I unlocked and did a few reps at 150 pounds. Each time letting my shorts slide higher and higher up my thighs, knowing at any given moment my uncut cocks could possibly be revealed if he was looking hard enough. It turned out from his vantage point he must not have been able to see. So I changed up my game plan.

"Hey, bro, can you throw on two more 50's?" I called out after taking out an ear bud.

"SURE!"

I tried not to smile, he'd been paying such close attention he jumped up immediately.

I watched him eagerly rush over and grab a plate off the

rack and move over to the machine and start putting them on. After getting the second plate on I smiled.

"Thanks, could you stick around and spot me?"

He smiled and nodded.

I didn't need a spotter. The machine comes with safety locks that you can engage with your hands and the machine only drops so far down. He clearly wasn't paying attention to that. So I went back into my routine and with each press squeezed my thighs as tight as I could and felt my right dick slip into view. It was obvious because I noticed him looking at it. I can't explain it, but the second I feel someone's eyes on me like that, I feel a tingle deep in my groin. I smiled and pushed the machine up and locked it. He almost flinched when I spoke.

"Throw on two more plates?"

He stuttered briefly then put on two more, keeping his eyes almost totally locked on my crotch as casually as he could. Now at 350 pounds I cranked on through and near the last rep I felt my left dick pop out into view. Even if I hadn't felt it, his face gave it away. It was almost comical. His brows pinched together then his eyes grew wide and his face flushed. I finished that set and asked him to put on two more plates and watched him almost drop one as he moved to the left side and saw my left dick clearly. I ignored his fumbling and went into my second to last set. Sweating like a pig I slowly finished and paused after locking them in. I looked over and up at him.

"Put on two 25's."

He glanced at my face and smiled.

"Not bad man," he grinned as he added the last two plates bringing me up to 500 pounds.

I'm not sure if he realized I knew he was looking at them or not but he was a lot more comfortable staring at them. I went through the last set and spent the following fifteen minutes having him take weights off until I was down to 50 pounds and went through a burn-out set. I reached down and tugged the hem of my shorts down to my knees covering up my dicks and pulled myself out of the machine.

"Thanks man, I appreciate it. Usually I have to climb out and add on the weight myself.

He grinned and nodded and stood there as I walked off to the locker room. I smirked wondering what he'd do. The ball was in his court.

I had gotten my locker open and decided I'd go as slow as possible, give him enough time to build up the courage to follow me. I knew he would, and he did. I'd just gotten my shirt off when I heard the door push open and he came around the corner. He walked behind me and came around to a locker three down from mine and spun the combination a few times before giving it a jerk. He dug around inside for a few seconds then stopped. I stood there looking at my iPod when he spoke.

"Can I see them?"
I tried not to smile.
"What's that?"
"Can I see your, dicks?"

I laughed a little nervously, he blushed deep red.

"You've got two, I saw them when you were doing your leg presses."

I had to give him props, he was forcing himself to talk through a bundle of nerves.

"Are you gay or something?"

I almost cringed and felt bad saying it like that. It came out more like an insult than a question.

He paused and looked at the ground and only made me feel like a bigger jerk.

"I think I might be now, I dunno," he muttered without looking up from the floor.

I took a deep breath and grabbed my waist band.

"Okay."

He looked up so suddenly I almost told him not to give himself whiplash.

He watched in a glassy stare as I pulled my shorts and jockstrap down in one slow fluid movement. By then both my dicks were getting fluffy. His mouth dropped open and his eyes grew so wide I actually laughed a little.

"How is this possible?"
"Long, long story," I replied quietly.

Without asking he stepped closer and dropped to one knee.

"Did you have plastic surgery or something?"
"No, I was born this way."

He lifted his hand up then put it back on his knee and

then looked up at my face, bright red and almost shaky.

"This is so fucked up but, can I-" he started when I interrupted him.

"Go ahead," I smiled, his nervousness and raw sexual attraction was driving me wild. Little did I know what he was asking.

Without another word he took both my dicks in each hand and began squeezing and tugging on them. To say he caught me off guard would be a gross understatement. Now I was the one who was dizzy and flushed. I made a mental note, in the future let them finish the request before you say okay.

I steadied myself on my locker door and looked down at him as both my dicks became completely hard. Immediately I felt self-conscious as I watched him slide my foreskins down from the heads. I'd been working out for almost two hours and while it wasn't disgusting odor, I could smell my dicks. I know, the girls reading this just grossed out. Let me reiterate, my dicks don't stink, but after 2 hours in a gym, men get a certain musky smell. If a guy is uncircumcised that musky smell is intensified and I could smell my dicks like they were in my face. I almost cringed. Before I could say a word he threw me for another loop.

"Fuck they smell good," he grunted before plunging my left dick, then right one in his mouth, alternating from left to right.

Now for those of you thinking there was no way he was straight, I can tell you that he'd never sucked dick before. He was all teeth and being uncircumcised means that I was struggling to stay hard. It did NOT feel good. Luckily he stopped brushing his teeth with my dicks and started rubbing them on his face. The problem was he had scattered stubble and that felt like sand paper.

"You really need to ease up on them dude," I exclaimed as I pulled my hips back from him causing him to lean back and look up. I noticed he had a raging hard-on.

"Sorry, sorry, I've never done this before."
"Yeah I noticed," I laughed nervously.
"Do they both squirt when you come?"
"Kinda, sort of," I shrugged.
"I want to make them come," he grunted.

It was my turn to look shocked. I'd expected groping, stroking and maybe some sucking but not that.

"I'm serious, this is probably the only time in my life I'm going to have a dick... two dicks in my mouth. I want to make you come."

I'm not sure if it was the look of complete lust and sexual craving in his eyes, the fact that he had pulled his shorts to the side and his surprisingly large cock was standing at attention leaking precum on the locker room floor, or that he really was a lot more attractive than I had first realized. Actually it was all of those things combined that made my dicks go rock hard again.

"I got to warn you man, I shoot massive loads," I cautioned.

He nodded and looked at my dicks, twitching in his face.

"Will it taste bad?"
I shrugged and replied. "Does it matter?"

He grunted with a look on his face that said I had just really turned him on.

"Just watch the teeth and don't be so rough."

He nodded again and went back to sucking. I managed to close the door to my locker and lean back against it. He managed to get both in his mouth without much contact with his teeth. He realized though he could only really suck on one at a time. Every now and then he'd let go with one hand and stroke his own cock. I felt my prostate swelling fast and knew that it was only a few more minutes before I was going to blow my first load. He had started focusing on my balls and was massaging my taint when I realized if I didn't get him focused back on my dicks he'd find my asshole yawning wide open. It was prostate day coming up (I'll explain in a later chapter) and I was swollen almost grapefruit sized. When it gets that big, in combination with being a very greedy power bottom, my hole opens up. I wasn't sure how relaxed he'd be about my ass trying to gulp his hand if he decided to reach a finger back there. Even though I wanted to reach down and guide his entire hand into my ass I pulled his hand away from it.

"Just the dicks."

He nodded and went back to sucking on the right one while stroking the left. I felt my orgasm approaching and started to breath harder.

"You gonna'?"

I nodded and braced myself against the lockers behind me. He let go of my dick, catching me off guard. For a fleeting moment I wasn't sure what he was about to do as he stood up. It was one of those times when I thought I'd gotten myself into a really bad situation. Instead he pulled his shirt off and tugged his shorts off and squatted back down and went back to stroking and sucking me. I'd started to go soft from the sudden paranoia that he was about to deck me and I think he realized it.

"Glaze me bro," he panted between gulps on either dick.

I let out a moan as I realized what he was asking for. It was something I got off on. A moment later I felt the first shot rocketing out. I watched it shoot out and nail him on the right cheekbone. It splashed up and hit his right eyebrow and into his hair. The next few shots hit him in the nose and mouth.

"Fuck," he gasped as he licked his lips.

Watching him roll around my come in his mouth made the next shots come out even harder. Shot after shot hit his face, neck and chest. I looked down at him as he kept stroking my right dick, each creamy white stream ejecting and splashing against his chest. His tan abs were covered in long milky streams that collected in his dark blond pubes. I felt my knees growing week and tried to steady sweaty body as I began to slide down against the locker. He let go of his cock with his left hand and tried to steady me by attempting to cup my body behind my balls. Immediately as it happened I gasped knowing it was too late.

"Fucking hell," he gasped as his left hand plunged up into my ass causing the biggest stream of come to spray across his face and onto the floor behind him.

"Oh my god," he exclaimed as his right hand slowed. I tried to speak but the sensation was overwhelming. His hand pressing deeper made me even weaker in the knees. It felt too good to care if he was grossed out, I just watched his face as he stared in awe as his hand slid deeper and deeper.

Everything went a little blurry at that point. His face was a mixture of shock and confusion as he realized what had happened. He didn't stop and was oblivious for at least fifteen seconds of at least six large shots that hit his face. Before I realized what was going on he had let go of my right cock and taken my left one and started sucking on it. I could feel my load being sucked out as I continued to shoot streams over his shoulder onto his back. His left hand kept wiggling and turning inside me. I managed to reach down and push his arm out a bit until his hand was firmly cupping my prostate.

"Squeeze it," I gasped as he stopped and looked up.

"Squeeze it, that feels so good," I moaned.

He grinned, and I watched him put both my dicks into his mouth and then suddenly felt him squeeze my prostate. He squeezed almost harder than I liked. I let out a loud moan and he grunted then started gagging and choking as my come erupted from his nostrils. It wasn't until afterward that I realized the warmth I felt on my legs was his load spraying out hands free. I could have kept going, but like most men, after they come, their libido is shot. I reached down and pushed his hand out of my ass and he looked at it almost nervously. I guess he expected it to be dirty or whatever, but it wasn't. He sat back on the bench and looked down at himself.

"Fuck," he muttered.
"Thanks."

He looked up at me and then back at himself.
"Fuck, fuck fuck."

I laughed a little and pulled my locker open. It was just after 5AM and I knew early morning members would be coming in at any time. I glanced back at him and he was truly glazed, coated from face to knees like some sort of giant, muscular donut.

"Relax, it's nothing to get freaked out about."

He looked up at me and laughed a little.

"I'm not freaked out, I just didn't know I'd like it so much."

"Sorry about the ass thing," I exclaimed as I turned to the locker. I knew he was looking at it.

"Why is it so big and," he stopped.

"Loose?"

He laughed nervously.

"Long, long story dude. But thanks for not puking or anything."

"I don't know man, somehow it was really hot," he laughed.

"Yeah?" I asked as I bent over to pull on my sweats, looking back at him watching him stare at my asshole.

"Yeah, it's fucked up but it looks like a big used pussy, like the kind you see in porn."

I could tell he was turned on as he stared at my asshole just before I pulled my sweat pants up. His dick was already twitching.

"Easy there cowboy, people are going to be here soon and you look like the finale of Ghostbusters."

He looked down at himself covered in come and busted out laughing.

"Give me your number, if you want to fuck around some more," I boldly exclaimed as I took out my phone.

He cautiously gave me his number. I packed my bag and I waved as I left him showering off my loads. I wasn't worried about him telling anyone. It was pretty obvious he was not openly into men. He later admitted that no one would have believed him anyway. We ended up meeting a few days later and repeated the entire scene again. Only that time he fucked me after I came the first time. Like so many other guys before him and after him he said my ass was amazing.

It was probably a month before I finally took his ass, with both dicks and he came to terms with his sexuality. We saw each other a few more times over the months following our first meeting. After a while he moved away and last I heard from him he was engaged to a girl he'd met. I baited him that last time we talked, to see how loyal he would be to her. I was happily surprised when he said that as long as he was with her, he was only with her. He joked that he hoped she never found his stash of gay porn on his laptop though. I hope he's doing well.

So as you can see there was a lot more to it than I initially said in my AMA. This applies to a lot of the situations I've been in over the years. Next I'll recount the first woman I was with after high school. This one has caught some flack since it was first published. Thankfully a number of women have reached out to me since to tell me they were so happy to see it included in my book. They have experienced the same thing and enjoy the same kind of thing that I write about.

AT YOUR CERVIX

(A highly explicit encounter with a beautiful brunette woman.)

We'll skip all the boring details. I was at a party, it was Halloween and I had just gotten really comfortable with casual sex. This was long before the gym jock in the previous story. I had just turned 20 the summer before and was constantly horny. I was dressed as Tarzan with a chunk of suede I'd found at a thrift store and some leather cords. I had enough suede to make a front flap and a butt flap and just enough to make a pouch to put my dicks in. All connected with the tan leather cord I basically was wearing a G-string with a loin cloth over it. It fit poorly, did not hug my body and gave away a lot to anyone who was paying attention. It was exactly what I wanted. A pair of tan canvas sandals and a dirty blond dreadlock wig and I was good to go.

I'd been invited by a mutual friend who was a male escort. We'd met in an online chat and he had sold me my fake ID. I didn't want to wait another year to go to bars. He had an older male client who was so rich that money meant absolutely nothing to him. At least that's how it seemed anyway. I arrived at his home amidst a variety of guys and girls, most appeared to be hookers (both men and women) or in some kind of work that was adult oriented. Imagine a Playboy Halloween party, only much trashier. I'd been grabbed, pinched, groped and squeezed from the moment I got in the door.

I located my friend and we struck up a conversation. Apparently he had told his client about me and the guy was extremely interested in meeting me. He didn't know I had two dicks, but he had been told I had a special talent. I was fine with meeting him but the hooker/escort lifestyle wasn't one I really wanted. After the last sugar momma, which involved no sex at all, I wasn't game for the idea of going through that again, especially with sex included. Even more especially when I didn't know what the guy looked like.

I'd been hanging around the pool area when I noticed a gorgeous brunette girl standing off to the side of the bar looking at her phone. She was amazing. Perfect hour-glass figure, long wavy brunette hair, deep brown eyes and perfect skin. She glanced up and saw me looking at her and smiled at me. She was wearing a knock off of the Princess Leia slave costume. I figured either it purposefully was ill fitting, or she wasn't wearing any bikini under it. I soon found out.

I approached her and introduced myself. We exchanged names and then began to survey the party around us.

"I almost didn't even come, these types of things are always a skank and troll festival."

She was funny.
"Why are you laughing?"
"It's not my scene either really," I confessed.
"So you're not an escort?"
I shook my head "no, I just know a few."

She nodded and eyed me very bluntly.

"I just figured by your body that you must-"
"Have sex for a living? Nah, I just work out a lot." I smiled. "You?"

She smiled again and then shook her head.

"I'm just a model, I've done some nudes and got some attention and I was asked to come to the party to meet some producers."

I glanced around and laughed, "I don't think you're going to meet any producers that you will want to work for here."

She nodded and leaned in "Do you wanna get out of here?"

I definitely did. We worked our way through the people and out to the front of the house. I'd taken a cab, luckily she drove.

"Where to?" She giggled.

I honestly didn't care I just leaned over and kissed her. She squeaked slightly but kissed back. Breaking the kiss she started the car.

"My place is only twenty minutes from here."

I smiled and nodded, trying to remain calm. I didn't want my dicks popping out before we were in her bedroom. She'd already stared at my crotch a lot. I was sure she hadn't seen both of them but I wanted the reveal to happen somewhere other than her car. The last thing I needed was being ditched on the side of the road dressed as Tarzan on Halloween night.

She didn't make it easy for me either, she proved my suspicion right when she pulled the front fabric of her slave costume to the side allowing an unobstructed view of her almost completely smooth pussy. A thick landing strip of dark brown hair in the middle above what looked in the dim light like a very large clit with a dangly piercing directly through it. She noticed my staring and laughed almost nervously.

"I hope it doesn't freak you out."
I felt my eyebrows furrow and looked up at her.
"It?"
"My clit," she blushed without looking at me.

I looked down at it and then back up.

"It's a clit, what would freak me out?"
She blushed more and shook her head, "it's *really* big."

I grinned, "doesn't bother me at all," I reached down between her legs and rubbed it, realizing how big it actually was as my rubbing pushed the hood back and revealed what was at least an inch of length as thick as my index finger.

"Wow!"
"Yeah?"
"Very wow! That's an enormous clit!" I awed at its size as I tugged on it gently.
"Ease up unless you want me to run off the road," she moaned.

I sat there trying to remain calm for the rest of the ride. We got to her place and in the elevator I stood awkwardly trying to keep my boners in check. She stared momentarily then shook her head. Only a few steps inside her apartment I hoisted her up and carried her to a huge overstuffed sofa. I wanted to eat her out.

She was sopping wet by the time I had her legs apart. I realized, face to face with it, her clit actually looked like a little dick, complete with a head and tiny shaft. The piercing went vertically up through the shaft and out where the pee-hole on a dick would be. I gave it a tug with my finger and watched her squirm. Without warning I pinched the ring and slid it out and set it on the coffee table.

"I don't want my teeth catching on that," I grinned as I leaned in and took her clit in my mouth and sucked on it.

She went wild each time I increased the suction and used my lips to pull on it. The inch of thick, pink rigid flesh twitched each time I let it go, the more I worked it over, the brighter red it got. Before I knew what was happening she had started to squirt on my neck and chest. Having seen girls squirt in porn I had always hoped to find one who could. I had seen enough videos to know how to use my fingers. In one fluid movement I slid three fingers up into her hole and began working her g-spot causing her to soak my face. She put her hand down on my face and gasped for me to stop.

"I'm going to pass out, you have to stop for a moment."

I sat back on my feet and smiled at her as she lay there twitching, her pussy yawning open and closed. I knew this was the moment. So I stood up and cleared my throat. She opened her eyes and smiled at me as I untied the leather cord around my waist. The entire shebang fell to the floor and I watched as her eyes processed what she saw.
"You have got to be kidding me," she panted as she threw her head back then sat up and looked up at my cocks.
"Nope." I grinned.
"I knew something was up," she laughed "I saw your... right dick when I looked down at it in the elevator, under

your costume, and I looked over at your reflection in the mirror in the elevator and saw your other dick and kept thinking I was seeing things."

I laughed, she *had* seen them.

"You're not freaked out?"

"I don't know if I can take them," she blushed as her left hand went down to her pussy and began rubbing and shoving fingers in as she looked at my dicks close up.

"Let me do that." I knelt down and pushed her back.

After all the intense G-spot stimulation her pussy was yawning pretty wide. I took my left hand and gently slid four fingers, palm up, inside her until my thumb was pressing against the right side of her pussy. She moaned as I curled my fingers teasing her again. I took my right thumb and hooked it in the top of her pussy and gently pulled upward opening the orifice wider. She squirted a little and gasped as I tucked my left thumb in and guided my left hand in past the wrist. She let out a long breathy moan as I slid deeper. I came to a stop a few inches past the wrist, my fingertips pressing deep against the mouth of her larger than average cervix.

I knew at that moment was she could definitely take my cocks. First I wanted to tease her and I began to wiggle my fingers around, poking and teasing her cervix. I slowly drew my hand almost to the wrist and then pushed back in deeper each time until it felt like my fingers were pushing deeper. She gasped when I curled them upward making her abdomen bulge up.

"What, what are you doing?" She gasped as she looked down and saw her belly button raising up and down slowly.
"Fingering your cervix," I grinned.

She let out a long moan and held her hands up for me to stop. I stopped.

"Put them in, both of them."

I pulled my hand out slowly, watching her cervix follow my fingers out about an inch or two between her lips before sliding back inside. She was slippery and wet from all the play, even still I asked first.

"Can I go in dry?"

She nodded silently with her hands up to her forehead. I put my dicks together and watched as her pussy gulped them up in one thrust.

She let out a long deep moan and went into a sit-up position. I felt the depths of her pussy bulge down against my dicks as I bottomed out inside her. The sensation was amazing, I could feel her cervix pressing down against the tip of my right dick. Without even thinking I started thrusting, the urge to push through was overwhelming. Even as impossible as I thought it would have been, I wanted to be deeper in her. She began spraying me down, to the point where I couldn't imagine how she had any left in her. Each thrust slammed my dicks into the back of her pussy, feeling her cervix bounce off the heads of my dicks, watching her abdomen frequently bulge up then collapse. She howled and moaned the faster I pumped.

"You're so hot," I gasped as I grabbed her tits and continued to pound. "You like feeling my dicks hammering your cunt?"

She gasped and covered her mouth and nodded silently as I hammered harder making her moan.

"You want me to fuck your womb?" I growled as I ran my hands down her chest to her abdomen which was rising up and down constantly.

"Oh fuck yes," she groaned at the top of her lungs.

I continued to run my hands down until I felt her abdomen pumping up and down under them. I was sure it was impossible, but it felt amazing and the idea was extremely arousing. I firmly pushed down into her abdomen with both hands as I felt it raise up when I thrust in again. The sensation on my right dick was almost indescribable. It felt as if my dick had pushed through and was even deeper. She let out a howl as I swore my cock pushed through her cervix as I pushed down on her abdomen with almost all my weight. I immediately began to come. Collapsing against her she shrieked and squirted again as her body convulsed under me. I knew I was deep but I could have sworn I went deeper. We lay motionless for a bit until she spoke.

"Ow."
"I'm sorry."
"Seriously, ow, it feels like you're in my stomach."

She pushed against me and I began to roll to the side which brought a gasp and another moan as my dicks began to pull out. A flood of come poured out of her into the sofa cushions. As my dicks pulled out further I felt a suction feeling on my right dick. It made me flinch which made my hips jerk and both my cocks yanked out of her at once making her cry out. I sat up quickly.
"Are you okay?"
"My pussy feels so weird right now."

I looked down at it and felt my mouth drop open. Her cervix was hanging out between her lips. I couldn't believe it, it looked like I actually had gone into it, it was wide open and red resting against the sofa cushion.

"I don't know how to tell you this," I paused trying to find the best way to put it.

"What?" She sat up suddenly and cringed.
"You're inside out." I said it as calmly as I could.

Her eyes grew wide as she put her hand down between her legs and felt her cervix.

"You really did fuck my womb," she gasped quietly as she felt around.
"I don't think that's possible."

She looked at me and gave me the funniest expression.

"My fucking pussy is inside out and I can put two fingers in my cervix, and you think you didn't fuck it?"

I stuttered and then shrugged as I watched her push it back inside only for it to slide back out again. It suddenly dawned on me.

"I didn't wear any condoms."
"I'm on the pill, are you clean? God, I should have asked these things first."
"I'm clean, but do you think the pill is going to do any good? I mean it looks like I actually did have my dick in your uterus."

She sighed and shook her head and slowly stood up.

"This is so fucked up," she exclaimed as she looked at herself in the mirror.
"It better go back inside," she growled at me through the

mirror as she kept trying to push it back in only for it to fall back out again.

That night began an on and off friends with benefits situation that lasted for about three months. For those wondering, yes, my right dick was penetrating her cervix. It finally stopped sliding back out but we hooked up again and each time it fell out afterward. I did find out she was older than she looked. I've seen tons of other cervix since hers and only a few of them were capable of penetration. I'm not going to say it's safe, or recommend doing it. It's probably really dangerous and if the girl you're fooling around with says 'stop' or tells you it hurts, you better stop. Besides that, I will say that all the idiots on the Internet in forums and websites who say penetrating a cervix with your cock is impossible, well they're wrong. I've done it plenty of times.

Those cover the two instances I mentioned in my AMA that got some attention. The other one that got the most attention will come a little later in the book. Ahead are the most common questions I've gotten since I went public. Some of these may have already been covered in my AMA, some not. Regardless, they are the questions I continue to get, hopefully they will clear up some confusion.

EVERYTHING YOU WANTED TO KNOW...

Over the years a few questions have always haunted me. Asked by close friends upon first discovery, from sex partners upon first encounter and now the public. Here they are, the top ten questions along with the answers in what I will try to list as the most popular.

MOST POPULAR QUESTION: ARE YOU SINGLE?

As of the publishing of this paperback book, yes. I am single. Am I looking? Always. However I am not on the lookout for a partner. Meaning if I meet someone who sparks my interest, well who knows where it might lead. As I said in my AMA, if I'm not interested in you, you won't know I have two dicks. So I won't be joining eHarmony or Match.com as DoubleDickDude. Sorry. :)

1. Do both of your dicks get hard?
Yes. Throughout my childhood the left one would start to get hard first. The right one would catch up and get completely erect. Depending on how horny I was the left one would sometimes continue to stiffen and get hard too. Back then the left one rarely got completely hard, I had to be very horny for them to both get equally hard. However after

surgery I had in February of 2014, both now get equally hard and erect.

2. Can you pee/come out of both?

Yes. My urethra forks in the shape of a Y inside my body. Basically it's one tube that splits and goes off through the left and right. When I pee it comes out both, the same as when I orgasm. Originally I had a urethral stricture just above the fork in my left penis. It wasn't as big inside so when I would pee it would balloon, which hurt. Once the pressure was strong enough it would flow out of my left dick. When it came to orgasms, on occasion the left one would squirt, but most times the come was sucked out. The same surgery I mentioned above corrected this. I previously had a similar procedure done years ago that allowed me to pee easily but over time it had gotten pinched again.

3. How big are your dicks?

Before the surgery in February 2014 my dicks measured: 7"+ Right Penis and 6" Left Penis give or take. The left one forked away from the right. The corrective surgery for my urethral stricture also included separation from the pelvis, via suspensory ligament division. The ligaments that hold the penises upwards to my pelvis were cut to allow them to hang lower. The surgery also untangled a mass of veins that rested between my dicks. A silicone implant was put between my dicks and between my pelvis and shafts to space them apart and keep them from re-attaching. Once completed both my dicks are 10 inches long, between 6" and 6" 1/2 inches around the shafts just below the heads. The heads are roughly 7" inches around each. Soft they hang just a fraction over 8" inches long. This is a drastic difference from how they looked when I did my AMA.

4. Are you bisexual because you have two dicks?

Answering this one is difficult. Having two dicks probably opened doors for me in the sexuality department. I won't deny that. I think that half of our sexuality is a product of our environment. Meaning the people we grow up with, our friends, family combined with the accepted morality of life has an impact on what and how we develop. I think anyone with an extra body part as significant as a penis would experience life differently than most. It wasn't until a few years ago that I came to terms with this. I grew up with the understanding that I was special. I grew up knowing I was different. It wasn't until I got out in the real world, away from school, my peers and my home town that I realized that everyone else is different and special too. The guys may not have two penises, and the girls may have only one vagina, but they are still special and different. I think having two dicks gave me an advantage. Once I came to terms with them I realized they impacted my life a lot more than I first thought. I can say I am not bisexual because I have to dicks. I am bisexual and I have two dicks. The only way to establish if my plural penises impacted my sexuality is impossible. We'd need an alternate universe where I was born with one, or had the extra cut off after birth. Then we could compare. The bottom line for me doesn't matter. I am me, I am happy in myself and make no apologies for it.

5. Which do you prefer, men or women?

I think I already addressed a portion of this earlier in the book. However it deserves a bit more discussion. There are definitely people who will not like what I'm about to say. Everyone is bisexual to a degree. In fact everyone is a woman to a degree until that defining moment during embryonic development when the cells shift and the clitoris becomes a penis, the ovaries become testicles and you have a male fetus. The point I am making is, we are all bisexual to a degree. The strength or extent of this degree is dependent upon a variety of factors. Environment, social spectrum, religious upbringing, moral compass, peers and personal comfort level. I know entirely too many gay men and women who 'crush' on the opposite gender for one reason or another, yet they struggle with it because they identify as one way or the other.

I've met and had sexual encounters with easily 100's of men who identify as straight, yet they have ended up with one or both of my dicks in them. I know many women who identify as gay/lesbian who crush on men but try to ignore it. In fact I was crushed on by three different lesbians in my time. None of them knew of my dicks, but during an evening of heavy drinking admitted they could go 'straight' for me.

Beneath it all I wish everyone would stop worrying about who is gay, who is straight, who is bisexual. Why must we define people by their sexuality? Why does Billy need to be gay Billy? Why does Sally need to be lesbian Sally? Why does Eric need to be Bi Eric? Why can't they just be Billy, Sally and Eric? Society groups people into classes to feel stability and safety. In doing so they break the hearts and souls of people like myself who don't fit into either class. Only in the past few years have people started accepting bisexuality as a legitimate sexuality. I know bi guys and girls older than me who tell me about a time when they were bi before it was 'trendy.' I laugh but deep down feel for them, just as I feel for the men and women who were gay when gay was as taboo as bestiality. How they survived to make it this far boggles my mind and gives me the utmost respect for them.

With all of that said, I will have absolutely nothing to do with the GLBT-yada-yada-yada establishment. A small percentage has a grip on the fact that a larger, vastly more vocal percentage of the 'queer' establishment has not a single ounce of respect for each other, let alone 'society' in general. The 'fish' the 'breeders' (and any other derogatory name you can come up with for straight people) are their enemies. Yet at the same time, the transgender men and women are jokes. The bisexuals are still confused, the gay men who are amazing performers in drag are still tired old queens and the masculine lesbians are dykes. I went to a Pride festival once and saw everything but pride. I saw ridicule, condescension and judgement. Hatred from the chubbies for the twinks in their tighty-whities. People snickering about the transgirls "looks like fish, smells like chicken." From that moment I realized, this is not (yet) my community. Until equal rights and respect are given from within that community, they have no right to demand it from outside.

6. When did you realize you were different?

This was asked in my AMA and the answer remains the same. My parents always told me I was special. It wasn't until high school that I realized how 'special' and 'different' people are really treated. My parents spent so much time reminding me of how special I am, they stressed that I should keep it a secret so as not to make any other boys feel bad for having only one penis. They spent so much time and energy on that, they forgot that I would be ridiculed and made fun of if anyone found out. Jealousy is a really terrible thing. Jealousy can make monsters out of people. Jealousy can make enemies out of people who would otherwise be great allies. Jealousy has the ability to wreck entire lives and drive people to do things they otherwise would never consider doing. I only wish my parents had also explained that some people would be jealous and would hate me and give me grief because I was special.

7. You date men and women? Your AMA mentioned you are in a relationship with a guy and a girl. How does that work?

When I came out on Reddit in the new year of 2014 I had been in a committed polyamorous relationship. The couple had been dating when I met them and after a substantial amount of time passed as their friend, I revealed myself to them. Her boyfriend realized that he was bisexual, I was his first and instead of splitting they decided to see how we worked as a 3-some couple. We lasted for a substantial amount of time. However when I did the Reddit AMA it put a strain on our relationship. We ended up splitting up in February of 2014. We still speak from time to time, they are doing well and engaged. The split was not because of jealousy or feeling unloved. The split was based upon the lack of privacy. They realized to an extent I'm an open book and had no problem telling complete strangers the kind of things I do. They also were afraid people would find out my identity and our relationship would be exposed. Do I miss them? Yes. Sleeping (actually sleeping) with another person(s) was comforting to me. It took me months to get used to sleeping alone. I had to travel a lot to get used to being in a bed alone. Since they didn't always travel with me, I used that solitary sleeping arrangement to get accustomed to it at home, alone at night.

8. When was the first time you had sex with another guy?

High school... With my buddy. He has since asked me not to include it in the book.

9. When did you realize you are bisexual? How did your family handle it?

Senior year of high school. I'd had sex with my buddy and realized that I really enjoyed it. It was a curiosity thing that turned me on. After our first time we did things together frequently until I moved out of my parents house. I told my parents not too long after I realized I liked both. They were supportive and looking back, it's a safe bet to say that they didn't even really care at all. My mom was concerned at first that I wasn't planning on having kids. She wants to be a grandmother. When I assured her that I did plan to marry and have children she was fine.

10. It must be difficult finding condoms that fit. How do you handle that?

Truth be told, I do not wear condoms. I tried once or twice years ago and just didn't like how they work. I don't condone 'unsafe' sex. I guess it is shocking that I am 100% STD free and clear.

FUNNY MOMENTS

It goes without saying that living a life with two dicks has put me in some hilarious situations. I don't typically use the wall urinal in the men's room. Too risky. But on rare occasion it's happened.

"Dude, you've got *two* dicks!"
"Dude, you've got *one* dick."

He stares and blinks.

"You want to suck them or something?"

He looks up at me in shock.

"I think I do."
"Well I don't want you to, your breath smells."

I left him standing there slack-jawed... his breath reeked of fish. GROSS.

~~

Was at a party, walked up on a joke in progress.

"Which side do you dress, to the left or right?"

"Both," I replied without thinking. Everyone looked over at me.
"I've heard that one before," I laughed nervously.

~~

I actually scared a hooker once. Me and two buddies picked one up and when we got back to the hotel room...

"So, three dicks, that's $200 per dick."
"Actually there's 4 dicks." I couldn't stop smiling.
"I didn't agree to no gang-bang. Three guys is my limit."

I take my dicks out and she starts backing towards the door.

"No, I'm not doin' none of that freaky shit, forget it!"

She bolted.

Cute but ditzy blond I had sex with once asked.

"If they both come in me, will I have twins?"

I actually kept my left dick in my jeans once while this cute shaggy brunette dude blew me. He had no idea I had two. So he starts begging me to fuck him and pulls off his pants and rolls onto his stomach and puts his ass up in the air. One glance and I knew he was a power bottom. I whip out my left dick which had gotten harder than usual at that moment and after a few wads of spit, I shoved both in his ass. He howled and arched his back and let out a loud groan.

"What the fuck is going on?" He groaned.
"What do you mean?" I panted as I continued to pump them in his loose hole.
"It feels like you're stuffing two cocks in me."
"If I was, would that be a bad thing?"

He laughed nervously and went back to riding his ass back against my dicks. About half an hour passed before he wanted to roll over on his back. I let him and he was so out of it he didn't look down or pay attention. I stuffed both dicks back inside him and he let out a loud grunt and sat up. He looked down at his ass and I watched him trying to process what he was seeing. He flopped back on the bed and went back to moaning.

A few hours passed and I finished emptying my prostate into him. The mattress was soaked, his ass wide open and gaping. I tugged them out and went to the bathroom. A moment later he walks in as I'm taking a piss, looks down and sees them again and then looks up at me and full out faints right there in a pile of laundry.

~~

Just like with the brunette dude mentioned above, there have been a few girls who didn't pay attention at first. This time it was a bleach blond cutie who I'd met at the beach. She was laying on her right side at the foot of the bed with her right leg dropped down to the floor. I had her left leg up and was plowing her pussy with my right dick. She starts moaning something about her ass. After getting her to repeat herself a few times I realized what she was saying.

"I want it in my ass."

So I pulled out of her pussy and put it in her ass.

"I want it in my pussy." So I pull it out of her ass and shoved it back into her pussy (I know I know, don't lecture me about bacteria and germs).

Then she starts muttering about wishing she had one in her ass and pussy. So I oblige.

About half an hour in, right dick in her ass, left in her pussy she reaches down.

"How are you doing that?"

"If I told you I have two dicks, what would you say?"

She looks up at me.

"Right now I'd say put them both in my pussy."

I pull them both out and wag them at her, she gets wide-eyed. I stuff them in her pussy and she orgasms instantly. She then tells me to stop and to take off the strap on and just fuck her with my dick. I tell her it's not a strap on and she refuses to believe me until she grabs them both and suddenly doesn't want to have sex anymore.

"We should stop before you come or something."
"I already did, three times."

She looks shocked, reaches down and feels my loads oozing out of both her holes.

"I'm so going to hell for this." She put on her clothes and left.

~~

After a long night at a party, having fooled around with three guys and two girls, all at different times I'm preparing to leave when a slinky redheaded girl approaches me.

"Are you the dude with two dicks?"

I just look at her perplexed. Behind her a cute scruffy dirty blond dude I let suck me off for almost an hour, stands there looking sheepish with what was obviously dried cum in his scraggly attempt at facial hair. Either that or people thought he ate 24 glazed donuts while they were still hot.

"You ruined my fiancé, thanks a lot."

She storms off and out the door. He stops and looks at me.

"Thank you, I didn't want to marry that bitch from the moment my parents told me I had to."

He hands me a scrap of paper with his number on it.

"Call me, please, I want more." He smiles and walks out.

I called him later, he got more. A lot more.

~~

A dude was jerking me, not brave enough to suck me. So impossibly cute he made both my dicks hard. Without warning my first shots fired off and both dicks launched... in both of his eyes.

"I told you not to get too close."

~~

"I've died and gone to queer heaven."

"You said you were straight."

The cute corporate guy with perfect hair, perfect skin, sparkling green eyes said as he knelt in his suit between my legs holding both cocks.

"I am but I'm sure this is what gays would consider heaven."

I laugh and shrug. This was also a guy who wanted me to blow my loads on his $200 silk tie. I creamed the lower half of the tie which was hidden by his vest. Afterward he took off his pants and briefs and sat under me and demanded I let him put his face in my ass until he came. So I did. After he came, he ate it, then wiped all the juice off his face into his slicked over hair and combed it.

I laugh now, because there is no way that dude was straight.

~~

The blonde who screamed... then ran. I never saw her again.

~~

The 'straight' dude who creamed himself the second he touched my dicks. He bailed immediately after.

~~

The two frat guys who also claimed to be straight but had

assholes as big as mine. Hilarious.

~~

The hipster who swore he was straight but swallowed every drop. He belched and said "Anymore?"

YE' OLE' PROSTATE

So for those who kept up with me since my AMA you saw me move over to Twitter and Tumblr. Once I had the freedom to post as much as I wanted, with ease I started to unleash more photographs. This brought up the subject addressed in my AMA, my prostate. Which was brought on by my love of fisting. While I love fisting a person, I LOVE being fisted. The sensation is amazing. However it's more than just a recreational thing for me. It's become required. So as I said before, my prostate is huge. Seriously huge. While the average prostate gland is around the size of a large walnut, mine is roughly the size of a large lemon or a medium orange. This is due (apparently) to the fact that my dicks actually start as one penis and then fork, forming two shafts. The base shaft of my penis is very thick, I'd venture to say somewhere around 7 to 8 inches around if it could be measured accurately.

What a lot of people might not realize is that the volume of liquid that shoots out of a dick during orgasm isn't determined by the size of a mans nuts. A guy can have monster sized elephant nuts and shoot only a few tea spoons of sperm. Where a guy with small grape sized nuts could shoot a few ounces of 'baby batter.' What determines the volume of what doctors call ejaculate is the prostate. If a prostate is healthy and the man has a good diet and eats the proper foods and ingests the proper vitamins, he can make his volume larger and change the taste of it. Or if you're like me, (and no one really is apparently) your loads are massive because your prostate is way too big and you're libido is out of control because you have two dicks. So what happens if I don't come frequently? My prostate swells. When my prostate swells, it seriously swells. It's swelled so large it pinched my bladder shut and I couldn't pee until I came.

So how do I prevent this from happening? Have an orgasm and ejaculate as frequently as possible. I try to keep it down to 2 times a day. From time to time I can't do that and when I start feeling my prostate swelling larger than I can handle, I have to manually massage it from inside my ass. This started with using my fingers. My prostate would swell so large I could push a few fingers in my ass and immediately touch it. Pressing on it would cause the fluids to stream out of my dicks a lot like pee. In long continuous streams. But, it wasn't comfortable poking/pressing my unaroused prostate like a ripe grapefruit. That's when I started working more fingers into my ass until one day I realized I could get my entire hand in. That turned me on, combined with the massaging and prostate day was born. Whenever I felt the pressure and intensity inside my ass and my dicks would start leaking fluid I knew it was time to relieve it all. So, a little lube, reach down, shove the hand in and work it for a few hours until I had come enough times to empty out.

A few years back I started experimenting with toys. Fist shaped dildos, large, unrealistic dildos, huge inflatable toys and the like. However once I started traveling around the world I realized it was too difficult to pack these kinds of things in my luggage and not get the funny 'knowing' stares from the security at airports. That's when I started experimenting with other types of more readily available objects. Fruits and vegetables were my friends for a while. Leave a large eggplant or zucchini out in the sun all day and it gets nice and warm. But as with most things in life, the more you become used to something, the more you crave the 'first time' feeling. So I started looking for larger things to use. From large plastic water bottles, all the way up to my current and favorite 'toy.' A 2 liter soda bottle is my best friend. The various makers have different sizes and shapes and they feel amazing. I could hide one completely inside my ass if I wanted too, with room to spare. The best part is, no one gives you a funny look when you buy a 2 liter soda. As for lube, I don't need it anymore. Need I say more?

Over the years this has dramatically changed the look of my asshole. As a lot of people have seen, and as I've mentioned in the earlier portions of my book, my asshole has been described as looking like a 'blown-out pussy.' You can only stretch skin so far, for so long before it just won't go back to normal. To clear up any confusion, no I do not shit myself, or have crap falling out of my body in my pants. My anal sphincter muscle is very capable of closing and holding everything inside. It's just very easy to stretch open wide and shove a few hands inside. While it can clench tight, I can also make it yawn open huge and push the insides of my ass out to shocking lengths. Just imagine it like a body-builder working out his arms or legs. The muscle gets bigger, and is capable of more training. My asshole is the same, it's bigger, wider and stretches more, but it is stronger and capable of clamping down tight. The only thing that doesn't clamp down is the skin. I've been asked if I'd considered having some plastic surgery to trim away or make my asshole prettier than it is. I have no desire to change it and honestly, I'm proud of how it looks. I like having a bubble butt with a 'ruined' hole between my cheeks. I like seeing it on other men who are attractive and in good shape.

DOUBLE HEADER: MY LIFE WITH TWO PENISES

I'm a big supporter of being body positive. If you want tattoos, get them. If you want piercings, have them. Just be prepared for negative attention and ask yourself if you're capable of coping with it. Just because you like something you've done to yourself, doesn't mean others will. If you can live with that, go for it. Just don't demand to be accepted and get angry when people don't accept you. If you care that much about other people and their opinions then tattoos, piercings and other body modifications are not for you. For those people who can't handle it, don't look.

I don't hate anyone for thinking my body looks disgusting. I'm in fantastic shape, I work out weekly and at a glance I'd be considered the all American guy. I've got two dicks, a set of big stretched nuts and a huge asshole, big deal. I'm not bending over and showing it to old ladies outside the beauty parlor. I'm not forcing it into people's faces. I am however happy with my body and everything about it. If other people aren't that's fine. Just be respectful and chill out when it comes to being judgmental. Acting that way does absolutely no one good any good to be treated that way for reason whatsoever.

THE ORGY

You remember that time I had sex with six other people at the same time? Oh yeah that's right, you had to be there. Or did you? The fact is I mentioned this briefly in my Reddit AMA and it created a firestorm of reactions. Everything you could imagine from people calling bullshit, other people finding it impossible to fathom and still others saying how jealous they were. Then there were the ones who said it was disgusting and immoral. The reactions really were priceless and kept me giggling for months. I figured when I was writing this book that I had to include a more in depth (pun intended) telling of exactly how that all happened.

About a year before I met the couple I ended up dating seriously for a few years, I was going through a really slutty period in my life. There were weeks where I'd had sex in some way with at least one different person every day. There were days when it topped three and four people a day depending on where I was. The point is, I was getting laid a lot, by guys and girls. Without getting too crazy in the details on how I met these 6 people I'll just establish a bit about each of them.

The Guys:

Guy 1: Great body, European look, black hair almost long enough to pull back in a ponytail. Blue eyes, pale skin, fantastic complexion with very chiseled features. He had fantastic muscles, no body hair and monster uncut cock that looks a lot like one of mine with a massive amount of foreskin. His cock was very dark, tanned almost to a grey tone with very thick, actually huge veins all over it. It stood out on his otherwise pale body. His ass was perfection, smooth and muscular with an asshole that matched his cock in color and texture. He clearly had been fucked in the ass a lot as it would yawn open wide allowing a view deep inside the pink tunnel. When it would clench shut the dark grey skin folded over repeatedly. It would yawn and clench over and over when licked.

Guy 2: Average body, all American look, sort of disheveled light brown hair with a scruffy face. Bright green eyes, not pale but not tan skin. His body hair dusted across his chest, legs, crotch and ass. His cock was circumcised and of average length, probably about 7 inches long with a sharply defined, dark circumcision scar that divided the skin of his shaft from a deep olive tan and a bright pale pink. What stood out besides his cute scruffy face were his gigantic low-hanging nuts. They were easily as large as tennis balls and hung far below his cock. I'd venture to guess his nuts hung at least 8" to 10" inches down in a very thin hairy sack. His sack had blatant stretch marks on it that he admitted came from stretching his nuts as much as he could stand. The best part was his hairy, sweaty ass crack; it hid a thick tan pouting asshole that was capable of swallowing those big balls.

Guy 3: Lean body with a bubble butt. Dusty brown hair with platinum highlights that was shaggy around his face. Sparkling blue eyes, almost a constant blush to his cheeks and a gleaming white smile. His body was completely smooth. His cock was circumcised and roughly 8 inches long. The head of his cock was large, with a bright read flared head. Riding very low to the base of his cock, only about 2" above the base was a bright pink circumcision scar. The underside of his cock was lined with stainless steel barbells. The piercings went from the huge Prince Albert in his large piss-hole, all the way down the center of his shaft, down the center of his nut-sack all the way back to his taint where it stopped at the edge of a tribal tattoo that circled his dark gray wrinkled asshole. He could be double penetrated dry, without lube and was working on taking a fist.

The Girls:

Girl 1: Petite blonde with a full body tan. Brown eyes and smooth skin with perky natural boobs. Her pussy was smooth except for a tuft of hot pink pubes that she had bleached out and dyed hot pink. Her inner labia were massive, hanging large and following back to her asshole where the gray wrinkled skin of her asshole blended together with her labia. She loved rough penetration.

Girl 2: Medium brown hair cropped short, green eyes and no tits to speak of. Could be because she was extremely thin. Her body was almost wax pale and her pussy shaved bald. Her pussy was the only one like it that I had ever seen. No visible inner labia and her outer labia did not touch in the middle. Her pussy was always open. When she lay back and spread her legs her pussy opened wide enough to see all the way inside to the back. When penetrated her abdomen would stand up like a tent. She liked having her cervix played with and could take a finger all the way inside it. The best part was after being fisted for a bit she could push her entire pussy inside out.

Girl 3: Long wavy jet black hair with bright blue eyes. Pale skin with double D sized implants. Her nipples were huge and were pierced twice in both. Hour glass figure with a large ass. Her pussy was trimmed with a triangle patch above it. After an intense pounding her pussy would push inside out a few inches and stay that way. Her cervix could be penetrated with two fingers all the way in which she claimed to love. It also leaked milky fluid nonstop when she was turned on. She had the wettest and sloppiest pussy of the three girls.

We had all met up, some friends of friends, some new to the group thing. The orgy wasn't planned and everyone came with someone. I came with Girl 2. Girl 3 and Guy 1 came together, Girl 1 and Guy 3 came together and Guy 2 we met during the evening. The physics of a 7 person orgy aren't too difficult when you have a guy with two dicks. The fact of the matter is everyone ended up being fucked by everyone at one point during the night. It was when I was riding Guys 1 and 3 when Girls 1 and 2 faced each other and managed to get my cocks in their pussies. It didn't take much effort to get Guy 2 and Girl 3 to get on the bed over my face and fuck while I ate them both out. That was when I realized how sloppy Girl 3 got and how much Guy 2 liked having his nuts shoved up into his ass.

It feels strange writing much more than that. Everyone ended up coming in that position and afterward we were all exhausted. It definitely was one of my most favorite sexual adventures. No, it did not include a bunk bed, sorry to disappoint. If you were on Reddit you'll get the joke.

10 FAVORITES FROM MY REDDIT AMA

Some of the most fun I've ever had talking about myself was during my Reddit AMA. My AMA was ranked the 4th most popular AMA on Reddit of all time. I even beat Peter Dinklage! You can't imagine how mind blowing that is. So, the questions and comments came at me so fast I had a tough time keeping up. Some people swore I had to be switching off with someone else. They said there was no way I was the only person answering questions for over 48 hours straight. At least I think it was 48 hours. Anyway the point is, so many people still have no idea what Reddit is or how to find it. Since Reddit closed/archived my AMA and it's pretty difficult to find if you don't know how to search for it, I'm including the best of the best here. Credit given to the posters when available.

Diemac : I bet your dad won all the arguments if any other parent compared their kids to you. "well Andrew, my kid has two dicks. So Andy Jr. can suck it twice."

~~

InscrutableTed: Just to summarize what we've learnt. He's bisexual. He's attractive. He's lives in a threesome. He likes fisting others and being fisted. He likes putting things down his urethra. He casually mentions the time six people had sex with him simultaneously. He shoots 12 times when he comes. Straight men magically turn bi-curious around him.

And on top of that, he has two penises.

Well played, God. Good to know you didn't waste that extra penis on a prude.

~~

McNeese: Holy shit. You know no one else has ever done this, right?

Like... like you're some sort of sexual Neil Armstrong.

"This is... Two large dicks for man. Two... giant cocks for womankind."

~~

10ac: Did you have any nicknames in High school? Johnson & Johnson seems like a pretty good one.

~~

jtdc: Can you write your first and last name in the snow simultaneously?

Carmen: He's ambidickstrous.

~~

Maxsusful: Are you a time lord? They have two hearts, so

they might have two of something else.

~~

Daikar: Can you blow air through one and out the other?

~~

ZBeebs: So when you masturbate, how do you control the mouse?

~~

UnleashTheAgronox: Have you ever done this:

Step 1) Tell someone you don't know "I have 13 inches of penis."
Step 2) Offer to show them.

Step 3) Whip out penis number 1, to mild disappointment.

Step 4) Whip out penis number 2, for the Big Reveal!

Well, have you?

~~

santacruzer7: Does Professor Xavier really have a school for gifted youth?

WHAT STARTED IT ALL

Back late in 2013 I submitted some photos of myself to a blog on Tumblr that I was a fan of. The Meat Market puts up some pretty hot photos of guys being fisted, or having huge assholes. That turns me on (obviously) so after a while I thought, maybe I'll send them a photo or two of my dicks. In the electronic version of this book I failed to mention that my boyfriend had been bugging me about sending in photos. I had been hesitant about doing it but eventually he talked me into it.

Low and behold days later I was all over the Internet and on international news. For those who missed that I've been given permission to include the original questions that were asked that inspired the Reddit AMA. Yes, it's true, Reddit made me famous, but The Meat Market blog on Tumblr is where I first debuted. From that day on everything changed. Below, the questions that started it all.

<u>Double D: Your questions, his answers.</u>

1: Can you tell if someone is touching your left dick or right dick?

DD: Yes. If the left one itches, I know it's the left one, vice versa. If I'm getting both sucked by two different mouths, and one swirls their tongue around the head of my right dick and the other person is sliding it from side to side against my left dick, I can tell who is doing what.

2. How do you pee?

DD: Like anyone else. I take my dicks out, and hold them in one hand and point into the toilet. They aren't rigid unless I'm hard and I can squeeze them together. It's not rocket science.

3. Why do you pull back one foreskin in some of your photos?

DD: Variety.

4: What were your lover's reactions when you first tells them and show them?

DD: By the time I tell them, I usually have been dating them for at least a month. I don't usually have sex very fast and I've only dated 4 people that I had sex with. There were a bunch of one night stands, but those got old and I don't like how I feel after them. Plus those were usually the ones where people freaked out or lost their shit when they saw my stuff. lol

The usual reaction is different between girls and guys. Girls giggle and think I'm joking. Guys want me to prove it, immediately. Actually I replied once "right here? in Starbucks?" lol Usually its awe and amazement. If they've been with me long enough, they are considerate when they first see them.

5. Do you thank your parents every day for not having the doctor chop one off when you were an infant?

DD: Now I do. For a few years in my teens I hated it. As soon as anyone found out, or saw them, that's all they wanted to talk about, or they wanted to see them or play with them.

6. What do doctors and nurses say about them when they see them?

DD: It's been a long time since i went in for a checkup. because my left cock developed pretty damn perfectly after it forked off from the right one, there hasn't been many issues. every now and then my prostate gets really full of seminal fluid and has to be released. but either i or my boyfriend can handle that now that my butthole is large enough.

7. Your butthole is large enough to....?

DD: LOL Its big enough for a hand to fit into. My prostate used to get inflamed and irritated in my early teens. One of the side effects of having two cocks. For guys with one cock, the prostate makes the juice that carries sperm when you shoot a load. Like 75-90% of the jizz is seminal fluid made in the prostate. It makes that juice when you're getting horny and aroused. Stimulation from your cock helps that process speed up. Since I've got two cocks, the stimulation is double and if I don't orgasm and release it, it builds up. In the past I had to go see the urologist about it and he taught me about how to use my fingers to reach inside to press on my prostate so the excess fluids would come out when I orgasm. Years later it's pretty much my boyfriend or girlfriend or whomever I'm with, will reach inside my ass and squeeze my prostate while I orgasm every few days otherwise it will get swollen.

8. How far in do they have to reach?

DD: Just past the wrist.

9. Do you enjoy it?

DD: If you're asking if I like being fisted, yeah. lol I do. The squeeze on my prostate sends me over the moon.

10: How many squirts do you usually make when you cum?

DD: probably a solid 6 or so from my right cock, followed by dribbling from my left cock. But if I'm squeezing my prostate after a few days, about 15 or so solid squirts and it flows out through my left cock at the same time.

11. What's the most intense orgasm you ever had?

DD: In a 7 way.

12: How did that work?

DD: Two guys laid on the bed, balls to balls, and I sat down on their cocks, both in my ass. Then their two girlfriends had me lean back and prop myself up with my arms. They faced each other, pussy to pussy and put my cocks in them. Then another guy and girl stood over me, and he took turns fucking her ass, pussy and my mouth while I licked her pussy and clit and his balls.

13: That's, wild.

DD: Yeah, I can admit that one was one of the best.

14: Got an answer for us yet about what celebrity you'd like to show your cock to and have sex with if they were interested?

DD: Yeah I've been thinking about it. I've come up with a few, guys and girls. So, without a doubt, James Franco. I'd love to go "Hey man, you ever met a dude with two cocks?" And watch him look all confused and do that goofy smirk he does and him say something like "what? nah man." and then go "Do you wanna?" and yeah... I'm sure he'd say yeah. Then show my dicks to him and ... mmm yeah, I'd love to give James Franco a full glaze facial.

Jason Mewes. Because fuck, he'd probably blow me and I always thought Jay was hot in the Kevin Smith films. I'd love to DP Mewes' big jiggly butt while pulling his hair and afterward pull my cocks out and make him suck me off till I came.

I used to fantasize about having a 3 way with Jessica Simpson and John Mayer. I'd love to show my cocks to Kendra Wilkinson from that old Playboy reality show, the girls next door. Her reaction would be priceless.

And I guess, last on the list would be the middle dude from Hanson. I've seen tons of rumors and pictures of him having a big ragged asshole and that turns me on big time. would love to meet him and ask him if he wanted to fuck and then just raw-dog his worn out ass then double stamp his face. lol Just to say I did.

15: Reddit wants you to do a AMA (ask me anything) session, would you?

DD: Maybe. I read some of the comments on the link you sent me. so I'm already there. Just not real savvy on how Reddit works. tell everyone thanks for the support and kindness. I'll take more pics for you and send them.

Your questions & his answers:

1. Do you go commando?

DD: Commando usually, I don't like boxers and briefs aren't big enough to hold my cocks.

2. If you took unzipped your pants and showed someone, what would they see?

DD: I don't usually show and deny it when asked. But this pic is what you'd see.

3. Have you had a guy suck one cock while a girl sucked another?

DD: Yes, it's fun.

4. Is your orgasm the same if you jerk off both cocks, or just one?

DD: hard to explain. feels good stimulating both, but the harder one feels better.

5. Would you ever do porn?

DD: not interested in it. probably seems weird, since I've got two dicks, but just not into exhibitionism. the fact that I'm sending you pix is really weird for me. people think of it as a novelty but it's my body. I'm not offended by rude comments... just that sooner or later the cool will wear off and then yeah.

6. Do you like or have you been fucked in the ass?

DD: yes and yes. with men I'm almost always a bottom unless I get REALLY turned on.

7. If you could have sex with a celebrity, or show your cocks to a celebrity, in person with a chance to have sex with them, who would it be?

DD: THAT one I'll have to get back to you on. Never really thought about it.

8. What do you think people don't consider when they see your pics?

DD: that I'm a person too, it's my body, it's always been this way. I've always had two dicks, and it's not something you wish for. I used to want only one. school wasn't fun and I had to change schools a few times. Not saying any more than that. but I'm not ashamed of my cocks. I'm just protective of them. lol

---

Double D returns!

Okay so a few more questions answered.

1. Yes, both his cocks can get hard, the smaller one gets harder but it takes longer. His dominant cock, that pisses a bigger stream and shoots a majority of cum when he orgasms is the one that is the biggest and hardest.

2. No, he does not have 4 balls. Just 2.

3. Size: His dominant cock is roughly 7 inches, give or take how turned on he is. His smaller cock when at full size is about 6 inches.

4. Sensitivity: Both cocks are equally sensitive, but he thinks the nerve endings are more receptive in his dominant cock. He can jerk both off and says that he does on occasion. Usually he jerks his right cock and the softer smaller one flops around while he does.

5. Best sexual experience: A 3-way with a chick and another dude. From what he tells me, the dude was straight, but when he saw Double D's cocks he ended up playing with them and sucking them with the girl.

6. Holes: He's had them both in a girls pussy, and in a girls ass, he's had them both in a guy's ass. He's had them both in a girls ass and pussy at the same time.

7. Ejaculation: When he shoots his load, the bulk of it comes out of his right cock, some dribbles out of his left cock and he usually has to milk it out of his left cock afterward. He also said that once he pinched off his right cock while he came and the cum squirted harder out of his left cock.

8. Surgeries: He has no desire to have one of them removed. He did have to have one minor surgery in his teens to help the split in his urethra form more completely. It had been ballooning inside from pressure, where his dicks separate and they put catheters in him and did some minor surgery to make the intersection "Y" heal properly. So again, he can pee out of both dicks.

9. Public Bathrooms: Yes, he takes both out when he pees. Rarely uses a public wall urinal if he can use a stall. He always gets stares if someone glances over.

10. He is not single. He has a boyfriend AND a girlfriend. They know he's sharing photos and think it's funny some of the reactions he's getting. So, basically, hook-up requests are

not accepted.

11. He has no plans to submit video. A few thousand people have already shared and posted the pics he sent and he knows videos will just go even farther.

12. Absolutely, positively he will NOT submit a photo of his face. He does not want to be recognized on the street.

---

1. YES he can pee and cum out of both cocks.

2. YES they both get hard.

3. YES he likes men and women.

4. YES he has double penetrated both men and women.

5. It is called Diphallia, genetic condition that causes two penises to form instead of one. Only 1 in 5 million men have it and of those who do, only 1 out of 10 shows signs of diphallia like he does. Most are severely deformed, mutant looking penises, have inside out assholes and rarely do they survive childhood because diphallia usually is combined with other severe genetic disorders. So 1 in 5 million and 1 out of 10, would make him 1 in 500 million men with two penises this intact and perfectly formed.

Double D is back.

Also I passed along some of your questions.

1. He is 24 years old, about 6 feet tall 150lbs, dark blond hair, blue eyes.

DIPHALLIC DUDE

2. Why Double D? That was a nickname a buddy gave him in middle school. Obviously, it stands for Double Dicks.

3. Yes, he CAN pee and cum through both dicks.

4. NO, he does not have 4 balls.

5. He does not show it off. He says he's denied having two cocks a lot. The attention isn't always nice and he prefers to keep it quiet.

6. He has fucked women in both holes at the same time, using his dominant cock, the right one in the ass and his left cock, the softer one in the pussy. He has also fucked people with both cocks in the same hole. Guys and girls.

7. He is bisexual and for obvious reasons prefers men and women with loose or otherwise "big" holes. Looks get his attention, but personality is what motivates him to date. He likes well-proportioned women, blondes who are kinky. Men, he prefers well proportioned, or well built, muscular men. He says he prefers the kind of men that act or seem straight. He's turned off (usually) by flamboyant or extremely feminine acting men. He admits he likes twinks and very skinny guys from time to time.

8. Negative effects: Shaving. He has a difficult time shaving the hair that grows up between his cocks. He has to be extremely aroused for his dominant cock (on the right) to get completely hard. The left cock will get what is considered a semi-erection first but never get rigid. He likes tight jeans but hates that the seam rubs the skin between his cocks. There is a bundle of veins between them that bruise easily.

9. He can jack off his left cock, but it feels better to use his right cock.

10. He says men are more fascinated with his dicks than women are and some women have freaked out and refused to have sex when they see his dicks thinking it was a joke or a prosthetic. No guy has ever turned him down, even at the last minute.

TUMBLR FUN

The following are a series of questions that flooded in through Tumblr once my AMA on Reddit had concluded. These may seem repetitive but they were originally in the electronic version of this book and I felt that they should remain in the paperback version as well.

DO BOTH DICKS WORK?

Yes, 100%. I can pee out of both and come/ejaculate out of both.

—

HOW BIG ARE THEY?

After some minor corrective surgery this past February, they are now equal in size. Roughly 10" (inches) long when hard. 8" inches soft. Shafts are about 6" 1/2 around, heads around 7" around.

—

DO YOU HAVE 4 BALLS/NUTS/TESTICLES?

No, just two, shocking right?

—

IS ONE CUT/CIRCUMCISED AND THE OTHER UNCUT?

No, they are both uncut and I have A LOT of foreskin. ;)

—

WHY DON'T YOU GET ONE CIRCUMCISED SO WE CAN ALL KNOW THE ANSWER, WHICH IS BETTER, CUT OR UNCUT?

You cut something off your body just to satisfy other people and tell me how that goes.

—

CAN YOU COME MULTIPLE TIMES?

Yes, whichever one I start with, after I come I can use the other immediately and keep going. Then switch back and keep going. I can go a few hours, having orgasms roughly every five to 10 minutes.

—

DO YOU KNOW ANYONE ELSE WITH TWO DICKS?

No. I've read about some though. But I'm the only guy I know who has two dicks.

HAVE YOU EVER PUT BOTH IN A GIRL? YOU KNOW, ONE IN THE PINK, ONE IN THE STINK?

Yes, many, many times. Also have put both in the pink, or both in the stink. Same for guys.

DO STRAIGHT GUYS LIKE YOUR COCKS AS MUCH AS YOU CLAIM?

Yep, at least the ones who've seen them in person. My cocks are like a unicorn or … in my case a magical ram. ;)

WHY DIDN'T YOU GET THE EXTRA ONE CUT OFF?

Why? They both work. I may call the right one my dominant one, but the truth is, doc's weren't sure which one actually WAS the dominant one.

ARE YOU BISEXUAL? DO YOU ACTUALLY SUCK DICK?

Yes, I'm bisexual and I LOVE sucking dick. But I also love eating pussy. One of my favorite things to do is sucking a guy's dick while he's fucking a pussy. Tasting pussy on cock really turns me on. Eating cum out of a pussy is just as amazing.

DO YOU THINK HAVING TWO COCKS MADE YOU BISEXUAL?

I don't think so. I've had 2 all my life so trying to imagine how I would've turned out otherwise is tough to do.

—

DO YOU SHOW IT OFF IN PUBLIC, LIKE IN A BATHROOM OR LOCKER ROOM?

No. In bathrooms I use the stall if at all possible. Regardless of what people think, guys DO look. It's denial when guys say no one looks, some people do. I know, because it's happened to me. Since I can't internally control which dick the pee comes out of I have to take both out.

—

WHY DON'T YOU DO PORN?

There is no price tag on my dignity. In that environment you go from being unique to becoming a novelty. I have no desire to exploit myself in THAT way. When it came to taking photos of my cocks and posting them on the Internet... I did it because, without them, no one would believe it. Plus I felt it was worth educating people that this exists and it's not freakish or unfortunate.

—

HOW CAN YOU DATE TWO PEOPLE? DOES ONE OF THEM EVER GET JEALOUS? HOW DOES THE SEX WORK?

There's a special kind of understanding that is required to manage a 3-way relationship. Communication is key, even if you think it might make things difficult. It's always better to be honest and open because then no one has the chance to assume anything. Neither of my partners have gotten jealous and I have never been jealous of the two of them. They were together before they met me. My boyfriend realized he was bisexual once it was revealed that I have two cocks. It's pretty lengthy to explain it all. As for sex between the three of us, I'm not willing to go into details as that is personal. However we satisfy each other and there has yet to be any problems.

—

SOME PEOPLE SWEAR YOUR PHOTOS ARE FAKE AND WANT YOU TO POST VIDEO. YOU SAID YOU WON'T POST VIDEO. SO THEY CONTINUE TO DOUBT YOU HAVE TWO COCKS. HOW DOES THAT MAKE YOU FEEL?

It doesn't bother me at all. My anatomy requires no one's belief in it to exist. I have no desire to make videos, my photos are plenty. Besides, what I feel is the most important thing at this point is the message, the knowledge and understanding I hope to inspire. Drooling over my dicks was never the purpose for going public with them.

—

WILL YOU EVER POST A PHOTO OF YOUR FACE?

No, absolutely not. I've seen a lot of reactions to this. Some are respectful, some are angry, some are disappointed. There are some things that simply cannot be understood. To understand how having two cocks can impact your life (besides the physical/sexual aspect) you must have two cocks. There are a lot of people (mostly men) who believe that having two cocks would make their life great. It did not make mine great. When it was revealed in my last two years of high school, it made life hell. Once I graduated I went on a rebellious streak and 'owned' my cocks. I was very open about it and everywhere I went, I was no longer ME. I was the guy with two cocks. Half of the attention was disbelief (which was accompanied by a demand for proof), the other half were assumptions.

No matter what I said or did, I was still just the guy with two cocks. The only way I can put it that might click with most people is the dichotomy of Clark Kent and Superman. If he had revealed he was Clark and vice versa he would never have had a moment of personal time. We all saw the kind of grief he and Lois experienced, and only she knew. If he had revealed himself, everywhere he went people would expect things, or assume whatever. Anything not spelled out, would be filled in by the individuals assumptions. Every action would be perceived as motivated by the secret. He would never have had 'down' time. To be honest, having two cocks does not make up for every single shred of my privacy being obliterated. It does not make up for being judged one way or another. People set up expectations of a person based on what they know. My two cocks are a part of me, they aren't all I am.

—

WHY DID YOU DO IT? WHY DID YOU GO PUBLIC? AFTER ALL THIS TIME?

There's a ton of judgment and ridicule against people for things they cannot control. Deformities, medical abnormalities, mental conditions and a variety of other handicaps. There are tons of people who have to keep something secret because if anyone knew, it would change their life, and not always for the better. There are people who live in fear of what others may think. Someone needed to tap the fishbowl of the world and get everyone's attention. I thought, you know? I can get their attention, and manage it in a way that will keep me safe. I can get their attention and try to make a positive difference.

I can't tell you how many fantastic comments, messages and notes I've gotten since my Reddit AMA. People who said things as small as "You made me laugh, thank you." To "You made me feel like I could go another day." And "I feel better knowing you are alive in the world right now." Some of it was detailed and 90% of those messages had very little to do with my body and more to do with my attitude and thoughts on things. I made people feel better, I made someone rethink something, I made it easier for someone to come out. I reached someone who felt no one else could understand them.

THOSE are the reasons I did what I did.

MORE FUN ON TUMBLR

Some of the funniest questions and reactions have come from my Tumblr followers. All the questions/comments included were given permission for public viewing by the user. Here are some of my favorite questions and my answers:

nplnpr asked: Do you keep a list of people you have fucked with the right dick and another list with the names of people you have fucked with the left dick?

Me: No, I'm trying to SAVE the trees here.

—

wolfayal asked: Hey DDD. I tried to shoot you a tweet a few days ago, but that was before I knew twitter ate it. Anyway I just wanted to say that I really loved the AMA and your whole attitude to everything. Thank you for being confident enough to share with the world. I'm a transman and while I'd be happy to have even -one- cock, let alone two, reading about you has given me hope that one day I'll be able to have one without surgery. Thank you again and just keep on being you!

Me: Thank you for the kind words. Soldier on my good man! You're unique and handsome! xo DDD

—

curtisellis89 asked: You said you're in a polyamorous relationship. I was wondering do all three of you guys live together? And how long have you guys been a trio? My partner and I tried a poly relationship but it just didn't work for us. I think it was because who we tried it with. Anyways I was just curious.

Me: We do share living space. The rule from the beginning was/is communication. No matter what, always communicate. Some people aren't cut-out for it and shouldn't try it. We three have done pretty well for a while now. Only time will tell though. As a rule we don't treat it like a concrete situation and are mindful that it could change at any time. We're currently happy but don't blindly believe it could always be that way. People change and we admit anything is possible. It keeps things going smoothly.

—

royibex asked: This isn't a question. I personally want to think you for coming forward and the fact that you own and embrace your uniqueness is utterly amazing and very inspirational for others that have been dealing with their own body "issues" I personally don't have anything that lets me stand apart but I do with patients dealing with psoriasis and I know how they struggle having to explain things to people they might encounter. So thank you for being you!

Me: Thank you. It's one of the main reasons I decided to do this. :)

---

cerolobo asked: Where are you from?

Me: Krypton. ;)

---

mancunts asked: Okay, not a question, but I just wanted to comment on your level of maturity in dealing with this sensitive and understandably deeply personal issue. You are to be commended. And thank you for sharing this portion of your life with us. Maybe this will help others with body issues to learn to love and accept themselves for what they are. I wish nothing but the best for you and your lovers.

Me: Thank you! That's really what I hope the end result will be of all of this. Acceptance, compassion and self-confidence for everyone.

---

nsaria05 asked: I'm fascinated by how casual you are about fisting, most guys flip out about it. First of all, what made you realize that that was a good thing for you, and second you've stated that you can take a double fist but how deep can you go?

Me: People get freaked out for two reasons usually. 1. They are afraid of what others will think. 2. They don't understand the act itself.

I can't remember how much of it I covered in my FAQ, but ultimately it began because of mandatory prostate stimulation to relieve buildup of excess seminal fluids. My body doesn't recycle/absorb the fluid as fast as the average guy and my prostate is massive by comparison to the average guy. So to relieve swelling manual massage is required from time to time. What started as a finger, turned into two, then after a while, an entire hand and so forth. ;)

I can take two fists up to around the elbow. I've had 3 to 4 hands in my ass just around the wrist.

Really what everyone should get out of this (besides the obvious) is that you shouldn't be concerned about what other people think about you or what makes you happy. You may not like it or find it appealing but that's no excuse to be rude or ignorant about it.

Thanks for asking. :) DDD

—

Anonymous: Did you ever meet James Franco? If so, did you two fuck?

Me: No I did not meet up with James. However I did get some 'intel' through the grapevine that he saw my AMA and was flattered about my attraction towards him. I will say this, if I had met up with James and we had fucked and he had told me not to tell anyone, I'd honor his request. ;)

—

Anonymous: What was it like when Kevin Smith and Jason Mewes talked about you? Did you freak out?

Me: I was fan-girling like a bitch. Seriously, Kevin Smith is amazing and Jason Mews is so hot. It was exciting.

———

Anonymous: How does it feel knowing a lot of celebrities have seen your dicks?

Me: Kind of funny I guess. Back when it all happened my significant others started listing off celebs they were betting had seen and it was making my head spin.

NOTES FROM DDD

One of the things I took time to do back in January of 2014 was hand write inspirational notes and post them for my followers on Twitter. After a while I felt like the effort wasn't appreciated so I stopped. Here are the few I did post, in text form.

Embrace yourself.

Wrap your arms around yourself and squeeze.

If you feel better, you did it right.

~~

If you let someone steal your happiness, then you are an accessory before the fact.

~~

Opinions, worded carefully can mimic facts. Don't confuse the two.

~~

When life gives you two cocks...
make protein shakes!

~~

Tired of being alone?

Ask yourself this:

Are you being the person,
that the person that's right for you,
wants to be with?

~~

True beauty can only be seen with the heart.
Close your eyes and be inspired.

~~

Always remember, you *are* special.
No matter what they say.

IN CLOSING...

So there you have it, the print version of my first writing endeavor. I did a little cleanup of it so it should be a lot easier to read. I'm sure it's not nearly as interesting as you might have hoped. Unfortunately because of privacy issues a lot had to be edited out. If I was openly/public about my condition there would likely be more in this book. But now that we're at the end I find myself trying to imagine the thoughts running through your head.

Why did he write it?

What is he hoping to accomplish with it?

I can tell you I decided to write this when I saw how many people really were impacted by my presence on the Internet. It was the last thing I expected. Sure I figured there would be the obligatory gawking and linking and sharing of my photos. I knew some people would be curious about it all. I had no idea though that after the fact people would still care. I began my Reddit on Jan 1st 2014 and as of this paperback formatting and editing writing there are is only a week or two left in 2016. Nearly a two years have passed and every day I still get messages from people. Besides the requests to hook-up or go out on a date, there are so many messages from people who feel connected to me somehow. Either emotionally because of something I said, or just because I made them laugh.

The point, now that I am at the end of the book, has become clear. I wanted to put more of a voice to the man with two dicks. I've shared photos on my Tumblr and Twitter pages, my notes from DoubleDickDude, featured earlier in the book were tidbits from my heart and soul. The fact is we are all special, even if you don't have two dicks, or just two boobs, or one pussy; you're special. You're as special as I am, we're all equally special. We have to remember that when the day is over, and we're falling asleep, we're all human. We all have hopes and dreams. We all aspire to something. We all have feelings. While I may have two dicks, I have feelings just like any guy with one dick. I worry about a lot of the same things and I'm no better because of my body. Regardless of my muscles, my dicks etc., I am just unusual. We all have things that set us apart but under it all there are more things that make us similar.

So after you've finished reading this, you might glance at a guy here and there with a large bulge or maybe even two bulges and wonder if he is DoubleDickDude. You might see me, walking down a busy sidewalk, in a crowded subway car, on the beach or on a plane. Or you may never ever see me. The point is, I exist, you exist, we all exist and we're all in this together, let's try to make it a little easier on everyone and remember to be kind.

Take care my friend, and like Superman told Lois...

I'm always around. ;)

DDD

Made in the USA
Monee, IL
10 January 2022

88621752R10062